HONESTLY

HONESTLY

SHEILA WALSH

ZondervanPublishingHouse
Grand Rapids, Michigan

A Division of HarperCollins*Publishers*

Honestly
Copyright © 1996 by Sheila Walsh

Requests for information should be addressed to:

📘 ZondervanPublishingHouse
Grand Rapids, Michigan 49530

Library of Congress Cataloging-in-Publication Data

Sheila Walsh, 1956–.
   Honestly / Sheila Walsh.
      p. cm.
   ISBN: 0-310-20325-2 (hardcover)
   1. Sheila Walsh, 1956– 2. Christian biography. 3. Entertainers—Religious
life. 4. Depressed persons—Religious life.   II. Title.
BR1725.M449A3 1996
248.8'6-dc 20
                                            95-45383
                                                CIP

International Trade Paper Edition 0-310-20835-1

This edition printed on acid-free paper and meets the American National
Standards Institute Z39.48 standard.

Published in association with Wolgemuth & Associates, Inc., 330 Franklin
Road #135A-106, Brentwood, TN 37027.

Edited by Evelyn Bence
Interior design by Sue Koppenol

Printed in the United States of America

98 99 00 01 02/❖ DC/ 24 23 22 21 20 19 18 17 16 15 14

With love and gratitude to my friends
Steve and Marilyn Lorenz

☙

CONTENTS

FOREWORD

Strong.

I've always thought of that word whenever I've run into Sheila Walsh. The first time was in Holland in 1983; her hair was spiked, her jacket was leather, and her style of music was as direct and straightforward as the gaze in her eyes. From there, I encountered Sheila now and then at conventions, conferences, or even on "The 700 Club." I noticed her style, whether in music or manner, softened over the years, but she still seemed to exude that same strength, that same resolve to live life straight-ahead. Pure and upright. Controlled. Strong.

I liked Sheila Walsh. And I was glad she was so high-wattage. I remember hearing her sing and thinking, *What power, what clarity in her voice. What a gift to be able to reach the rafters with those high notes!* I also remember being interviewed by her on her television show and thinking, *What intelligence, what thoughtfulness in her questions. May God bless this woman who's doing so much to reach so many.*

And then, like you, I heard the news. This high-powered woman who seemed to live life so vertically with the Lord, who seemed so direct and upright, had been admitted into a psychiatric ward. I remember hearing the news and thinking, *What a shock, what a loss.*

I lost track of Sheila at that point. I heard she finished her rehabilitation and was in southern California. Someone told me he had seen her with books in arm at his seminary. I smiled. It was good to know that the broken pieces of her life were beginning to come together, and I thanked God she was recovering. I smiled again because I, if anyone, knew what it was like to come through rehabilitation and recovery.

That's why the next time I saw Sheila, a different and even better word came to mind. Gentle. More so, *broken* and gentle. A mutual friend of Sheila's and mine had arranged for her to come and speak to our office staff at JAF Ministries. As I watched Sheila stand before our group and begin to tell her story, I breathed a prayer of relief and gratitude. She described her experiences in the psychiatric unit and said, "I never knew God lived so close to the floor."

This was a different Sheila Walsh. And yet, the same. She still had power and clarity in her voice. She was intelligent and thoughtful. But strong? No, she was weak. It was Christ who, through her weakness, looked so straightforward and dynamic. Our staff was deeply impressed with the firm yet tender tone behind her singing and message. *That's what happens to people who fall flat, face down on the floor,* I thought. *Jesus becomes, oh, so potent in their lives.*

I see it every day in our ministry to people with disabilities and their families. I see him time and again fill and flood with force the hearts of broken people who have "hit the floor." And every time I see it, my own heart is warmed, and I'm reminded that I, too, "can do everything through him who gives me strength."

This is what Sheila's book, *Honestly,* is all about. It is gentle but disconcerting; poignant yet very powerful. In fact, I earmarked more than a few pages where, after having read of her fears and faults, I thought, *That's me. She's talking about me.* And you will say the same. You will start into a page all dressed up strong and confident, pure and upright. Then by the next page, you will realize your need to have God keep breaking you so that his strength, not yours, keeps shining through.

So be prepared to dog-ear a few pages as you begin this special journey with Sheila. And be prepared to live life a little more honestly by the time you finish her book, knowing more fully that living life close to the floor is an open invitation to be strong in his strength.

Joni Eareckson Tada
President, JAF Ministries

Part 1
The Volcano

On the edge of a volcano
I have lived for many years.
Now it seems the distant rumble's
getting louder in my ears.
I have tried to walk away
from broken pieces of the past,
but their edges tear my feet
like shattered glass.
I have tried to push disturbing thoughts
beyond the reach of man.
I have tried to burn my bridges
but I've only burned my hand,
pushing things under the carpet
hoping that they'll go away,
but I know I'll
lose my balance
any day.

1

The Distant Rumble

The weight of this sad time we must obey;
speak what we feel, not what we ought to say.
WILLIAM SHAKESPEARE,
KING LEAR

It was a glorious summer morning in 1992. The sun was rising over the water, and the bees were beginning to hum. I went out into the yard to fill the bird feeder and stood for a moment in the stillness.

I saw my neighbor sail off in his little crabbing boat, and I waved good morning. I wondered about his life. He was always alone, and every day he set out onto the water, the first to ripple the quiet. A solitary life. My little white dog barked at a visiting duck, but the duck seemed unimpressed.

I drank in the sounds of the lapping water as it broke on the boat dock. I imagined for a moment that I was ten years old again, home in Scotland, standing by the ocean, my place of peace.

I turned my back on the water to prepare for the day ahead. I felt heavy inside, as if every bone in my body had turned to lead while I slept. After I showered, I took my coffee outside, and in the morning warmth I prayed, "God, please help me get through one more day."

It was a lovely drive from my house to the television studios where I worked. I left early enough each morning to avoid the rush of traffic. As I drove through the main gates of the Christian Broadcasting Network (CBN), I thought again how strange it was to find myself in Virginia Beach, as co-host of "The 700 Club."

My husband and I had moved to Los Angeles from England in 1986. My record company was based in L.A., and most of my concert touring was in the U.S., so it made sense for us to make this home.

I had fallen in love with this country instantly. I loved the hope that seemed to be part of the fabric of the people. I loved the freedom to be able to try new things, to find new ways of saying what I believe.

In 1988, Jackie Mitchum, the guest coordinator at CBN, saw me being interviewed on a morning show, a Canadian program called "100 Huntley Street," which broadcast extensively to certain markets across America. Jackie taped the interview and showed it to Dr. Pat Robertson, president of CBN, who was looking for someone to fill the position of co-host for their flagship show, "The 700 Club." CBN flew me in to meet with Pat and to audition for the position.

I had worked for three years with the British Broadcasting Corporation (BBC) in London, but this was very different. I was used to taping shows in advance, so that if anything went wrong, there was time to correct it. This was a live show, and because it was live, it was hard to rehearse. The afternoon I arrived, the producer enlisted the help of a secretary for me to "practice on."

The next morning was the real thing. I was taken to makeup at 7 A.M. and by the time I left, my face felt as if it were three times its normal size. I was definitely made-up! My hair no longer had an opinion; it was set in stone and larger than life.

Pat arrived a few minutes before the show started and prayed with six of us in his dressing room. Then we were on.

I was petrified. Within minutes it became apparent to me that I was supposed to be fairly fluent in world events. But, as I told Pat when he looked to me to kick off a discussion on the situation in Israel, "I know about as much about the West Bank as I do about the Bank of America!"

Despite the fact that I was obviously not the Scottish Barbara Walters, I was hired that day. A month later we moved from the West Coast to Virginia Beach.

I loved my job and the stimulation of discussing pressing issues with prominent church leaders and theologians. I subscribed to *The Economist* and brushed up on American history and world events. As a student at London Bible College, I had been constantly challenged to open my mind to the input of other believers whose experience of God was a little different from mine. I like to live with mystery. And now, every day, I listened and questioned as Billy Graham, Charles Colson, Chuck Swindoll, and countless others sat with me for a while and talked about life.

On the surface I had it made and everything looked fine—but I was not fine. I had not been fine for a long time.

Life, like a volcano, seems to offer early warning signals. Long before a volcano blows, there are signs that the level of activity under the surface has increased. Distant noises and rumbles become more pronounced. They say that animals are more tuned into it than we are and become restless and alert, sensing something's not right.

There were many areas of my life that did not always make sense to me. I loved my job. I loved being able to talk about the love of God to such a diverse audience every day. And I received hundreds of letters from viewers telling me how the show impacted their lives. I knew this was true, but sometimes I felt like a secondhand car salesman; I had a sickening sense that what I just sold people may not get them all the way home.

For example, many of our viewers were very sick and longed to be healed. I believed, and still believe, without a shadow of a doubt, that God is able to do anything. He only has to speak a word and disease is gone. But, at least for the moment, in America those miraculous healings are the exception rather than the rule. Day after day many people wait, wondering if this will be "their day." If it's not, they wonder what is wrong with them. Some people claim that if you have not been healed, it is your fault; you have unconfessed sin, or you are harboring resentment toward someone. I realize that the Bible is very clear on our responsibility to confess our sins to one another and to pray for one another so that we may be healed. But what do we say to the many people who love God passionately, who have done all that they know to do, and still are not healed? I'm afraid we either doubt their efficacy in confession, or we simply walk away and say nothing. How barbaric we can be in our perception of faith, how brutal in our pursuit of the miraculous.

It was a privilege to be part of a ministry that reached out across the world and affected the lives of so many, but I used to wonder about the viewers who watched from a wheelchair or a hospital bed. Was I helping them in their journey, or making them feel more alone? I once received a letter from a young girl who was losing her battle with cancer. She watched the show every day. Sometimes it helped her, she said, and other times she wanted to take her shoe off and throw it through the screen. "You show me people every day who have been healed and I thank God with you, but you never talk about people like me, who love God but who are dying and are trying in the midst of it all to live and die in a way that would honor him. We are part of the family too." Her cry for dignity and acknowledgment tore at me.

I realized then that there are no quick, easy answers for any of us—even for myself. I'll tell you more about that later, about the rumblings that preceded the volcanic explosion in my life. But for now I will simply say that my life blew apart, the volcano erupted, in 1992 as my marriage lay at my feet in shambles. It was over. I was grieving and I was angry and I was so sad.

At that time I also kept an utterly impossible schedule. Most weeks I was at CBN from Monday through Friday, 7 A.M. till 6 P.M. After the show was over on Fridays, I would tear out of the studio to catch a flight to wherever my concert was that evening. I would usually have a Friday concert in one city and a Saturday concert and/or speaking engagement in another. I would often get back to Virginia Beach at 11 P.M. on Sunday night, and Monday would begin the whole process all over again.

As I look back now, I ask myself why I never stopped to breathe, why I pushed myself so punishingly hard. A large part of it was simply that at those moments when I would stand onstage and talk about the love of God, I felt alive, hopeful; I knew that with God anything was possible. But when the lights went down and the people went home, I felt powerless to grasp hold of those truths for my own life. I could see dimly where I was, and I knew where I wanted to be, but I had no map to get there.

At times I tried to arrest the manic pace of my life, but it's hard to stop a train that is moving so fast. It's easier to just hold on tightly.

By the spring of that eventful year, I knew I was losing my hold. I felt numb and old and distanced from people. I would wake up in a hotel room on a weekend when I was traveling and wonder where I was. Sometimes I would be physically sick before I could pull myself together enough to get ready for a concert.

When I wasn't working, I resorted to an old, familiar habit—walking the beach. When I could get there on a sunny summer day, I'd be surrounded by children in swimsuits, dogs with Frisbees, and radios blaring the latest songs. But I was cold inside, as if a damp, heavy blanket had been wrapped around my shoulders, its winter breath seeped into my bones. My thoughts were slow and labored.

I wasn't eating much at all. I would come home from work and lie in a dark room, but I could not sleep.

Sometimes, when I couldn't sleep, I would walk for miles along the beach at five or six o' clock in the morning. But though I was surrounded with beauty, with glorious sunrises over the ocean, I was numb inside. I would pray a prayer that was becoming increasingly familiar to me, "Lord, please hold me. I'm falling into a dark well." In my journal I wrote, "I feel as if I am disappearing a little more every day. I am so angry inside that I am afraid of myself. I feel so alone."

I felt as if I were slowly losing my mind. Although I was still functioning on the show, I knew that my distress was beginning to show. One morning as I was listening to a guest I was interviewing answer a question, I found myself staring at her. I didn't have a clue who she was. I couldn't remember what I had asked her or what I should say to her next. Fortunately, I had some notes on my lap, and I quickly referred to them. The floor director must have seen the look of panic on my face, because she asked me after the show if I was okay. I said I was fine. I was too embarrassed to admit what had happened. It shook me, though, to feel so out of control. I didn't feel I could talk to anyone or laugh about it with anyone, so I tried to dismiss it from my mind.

A few days after my memory lapse, I started to cry as I was interviewing a guest. I could not stop. I wanted to lie down on the studio floor and just cry until I had no tears left, but I managed to pull myself together enough to finish the show and then locked myself in my dressing room until I was sure everyone had gone home.

That summer I received a letter from one of our viewers saying, "I do not know what it is that is causing you so much pain, my dear, but I can see it in your eyes. Please get some help. I am praying for you."

That letter is one of the most precious gifts I have ever received. Somebody noticed. Someone saw beyond the words of encouragement, beyond the smiles. Someone heard me. I cried for a long time when I read it. Here was an old woman struggling with cancer, taking time out to pray for me and tell me it was okay to go for help.

I decided to go home for a week in September. My family lived an ocean away, and I missed them very much. I had already scheduled vacation time away from the show, and I booked my flight to Glasgow.

⟨ঽ⟩

My mother was a strong link in a long line of godly women. She knew a little of what was happening to me, but I knew I had to try to prepare her for how I looked. I had dropped about twenty pounds, a significant loss on my five-foot-four-inch frame.

My mother had seen bad times herself. When I was four years old, my father had suffered a brain thrombosis. He died a year later. His absence was felt every day, but my mother filled our home with her spirit, her understanding, her faith, her love of life, and her wonderful sense of humor.

She had always been there for me. When I came home from school, I knew she would be waiting to hear all about it. When I was eleven, I asked my mother if she would pray with me. I wanted to make a personal commitment to beginning my own journey with God, even though I had no idea where that road would lead.

For a while I wanted to be a missionary in India. I don't think I experienced a specific call to the mission field; it just sounded like the ultimate sacrifice. I hated to be away from home, and I was petrified of snakes and spiders, so I figured such a visible, measurable sign would show God that I loved him.

During my teenage years I remember watching as a friend from church rebelled for a time, drinking and partying. The impact that had on me was a fierce commitment to be different. I would walk along the beach after church or youth group meetings and pray out loud, calling on the stars to be my witnesses that I would never let God down, that he could always count on me. That prayer became a theme for my life.

At nineteen I left Scotland to study at London Bible College. I thought I had arrived in paradise. They say that when you are tired of London, you are tired of life. Well, I was wide awake. I went to the ballet, the opera, the theater, all on student tickets. My seat might have been far away, but I was right there on that stage—I never missed a note. Though I drank in the atmosphere daily, I never forgot for a moment why I was there: I wanted to know God's purpose for my life. Still seeing the mission field as a woman's "most committed option," I joined so many mission prayer groups I often had to let someone else pray first to remind me what group I was in. (It's Thursday, it must be Africa!)

As time passed I began to see that there was a mission field right on my doorstep. As part of our evangelistic practicum I would visit other college campuses on the weekends. For me this was much more than a course I needed for credit. Some of my friends and I put a band together, and as I stood in college gymnasiums singing about my relationship with God, I knew I had found what I was created for.

When I graduated, I let the boat for Calcutta sail past, and I joined Youth For Christ as a staff member, traveling across Europe and the United Kingdom, singing and speaking the Gospel. *Here am I, a musical evangelist*, I often thought. *Lord, send me wherever you can use me.*

And he did. For the next ten years, I traveled all over the world, gaining an increasingly loyal audience. I released several record albums and served as host for a BBC TV show featuring contemporary Christian and traditional black gospel music.

The problem was, somewhere along the road I had lost my way. Somewhere I'd lost the joy of my salvation and my calling. I chose to carry my calling rather than let the One who called me carry *me*.

⁂

Now I looked out of the plane as we circled the green fields outside of Glasgow. I was home.

As I stood in the early morning chill at the airport, I drank in the sounds and the accents as I waited for my suitcase, the wonderfully comforting sounds that had surrounded me as a child.

I picked up a car and drove fifty minutes south to my mother's house in Ayr. I love that drive. The roads wind narrowly along green fields, over hills, past herds of the black and white cattle this area is known for. There is a point in the journey where you can first see the ocean. I look for it every time. When I see it, I know I am almost home. The Ayrshire coastline is so beautiful: sandy beaches, cliff tops that hold the remains of an old castle, seagulls, and salty spray.

I drove up the familiar road and parked outside my mother's gate. I knew she would be watching for me, as she always did, kettle boiling, ready to make that first cup of real tea.

When she saw me, she started to cry. I guess I looked worse than I realized. I had asked her not to tell people what was happening in my life; it still seemed too unbelievable to me. But over that first cup of tea, she said; "If you don't want anyone to know that something's wrong, Sheila, you had better stay home all week, because anyone who knows you will be shocked when they see you."

I began to eat when I was home. Mom made all my favorites: minced beef with peas in it, mashed potatoes, home-baked cakes, and piping hot tea. It was so good to be there. Our family pastor, an Irish man, came and spent some time with me and prayed for me. His gentle words and strong prayers were like rain in the desert.

My sister and her husband and their two little boys live in Ayr too. One night when I was at their house, David, their older boy, presented me with a chocolate cake he had baked himself. "You look ill, Aunt Sheila," he said. "This will help."

Mom and I walked along the ocean and drove over the hills and talked and talked and talked some more. I told her what a failure I felt like, that I was afraid I was letting her down. But that isn't how my mother saw me. She hugged me and wept with me. She told me to hold on to the Lord, to take each day as it came, and that she loved me. I would need her words for the days that lay ahead.

I had hoped a week at home with my family would be enough to strengthen me for whatever lay ahead. Instead, it made returning to my own home much harder. Being in Scotland with people who had loved me all my life actually made me feel much more vulnerable when I arrived back in Virginia Beach. Instead of feeling stronger, I felt weaker, like a mere whisper of a person. I couldn't sleep or eat. I felt overwhelmed by fear.

I quickly returned to my former patterns: I would wake up at three o'clock every morning, wide awake and afraid. Some nights I felt as if I couldn't breathe, and I would lie on my bedroom floor wishing God would take me home. "Lord, hold me," I begged. "I'm falling fast."

On the job and over a national grapevine, people were asking or surmising what was wrong with me. I had spent so much of my life measuring who I was by how other people viewed me. Now I was in a time of crisis, and many people wanted to know what was happening to me. How could I explain to people who called from all around the country what I was struggling to understand myself? I thought I was going to drown.

I watched my coworkers watching me. It was obviously very difficult for some of my friends at CBN to know what to say. Many of them simply stayed away. I was dealing with an overwhelming sense of failure for having let God and everyone else down, and I read their distance as an assent to my belief that my life was over.

All sorts of theories circulated around town. Someone had suggested to Pat that perhaps I suffered from manic depression and needed to be on medication permanently. Or, they speculated, was I simply a pathological liar, inventing all this emotional distress?

I did receive a few letters from friends telling me to get my act together. I also received one card that said God was not pleased with me. I hadn't seen this friend in years, and I was deeply wounded by his words.

I no longer knew how to do what these well-meaning friends were asking. I wanted so much to be able to pull myself together, but how do you hold a mountain in place when it is crumbling from the inside?

It became clear to me that I could not continue as I was. I was worsening each day. I was afraid to drive because at times I would lose concentration. At times I would find myself much further down the road than I thought I should be, with no memory of driving there. It was obvious to me that I wasn't thinking clearly.

All the while, in my purse I kept the precious letter from the woman who asked me to get help. I would pull it out and read it over and over again.

With every ounce of strength I could muster, I did reach out for help. Pat Robertson knew a little of my situation and had expressed a desire to help. I sat in the waiting area of his office and wondered what to say to him. I looked at the walls covered in awards and letters of thanks from prominent leaders and organizations he had helped. My heartache seemed to fly in the face of all the hope and joy these walls represented.

Pat opened his office door and asked me to come in. I sat on a sofa beside his desk as he fetched a cup of tea for me. He is a very busy man, and I knew that normally a secretary would do that, but on that day he took the time to make it for me himself. He listened as I tried to explain to him what was happening in my life. He asked me a few questions and told me how sorry he was that things had become so bad. And then he prayed with me. With tears streaming down my face, I listened as he asked the Lord to be close to me in the days that lay ahead. He gave me a hug and told me that his office was always open to me.

Several months before, I had interviewed a doctor who had given me his card at the end of the show, indicating that if I ever needed help, I should call. I had kept his card, and after I left Pat's office, I called his secretary to find out if he could recommend someone in my area. He suggested a doctor whom I already knew and trusted. After talking with this doctor on the phone for a little while, he told me he believed I needed to be hospitalized. He suggested a particular Christian setting in Washington, D.C.

This advice supported my greatest fear. My father had died as a patient in a psychiatric hospital, and I'd always wondered if I would end my days like him—in a place surrounded by strangers, tormented in my mind.

Yet I knew that the doctor was right; I knew I was beyond self-help. The doctor said he would check for the next available opening. I made plans to take a leave from "The 700 Club," not knowing if I would ever return.

When I told Pat I wanted to admit myself to a psychiatric unit he was very kind and fatherly, which is how he has always been with me. He made my decision easier than many others did. The day before I left for Washington, D.C., I had a conversation with someone who wanted me to consider the possibility that Satan was using me to try to attack CBN. I was absolutely horrified to think that could be true. I walked around and around the lake at our television headquarters, asking this man what he thought I should do. But he had no answers. He just shook his head. I was so tired I could not think anymore, and the idea that the crisis in my life was going to affect a ministry that meant so much to me was more than I could bear. I felt like a hypocrite. How could I sit on national television every day and tell people that if they put their trust in Christ, everything would be all right—when things were far from all right with me?

Those questions still weighed heavily on my mind when I went home that night, to walk the beach and pack my bags.

I'm fine; the sun is shining.
God is in the heavens.
All is well with the world.
I am dying; it is dark.
God, where are you?
Have you forgotten me so quickly?

2
How Do You Mend a Broken Heart?

*Woe to him whom this world charms from gospel duty.
Woe to him who seeks to pour oil upon the waters when
God has brewed them into a gale. Woe to him who seeks
to appease rather than to appall. Woe to him whose good
name is more to him than goodness. Woe to him who,
in this world, courts not dishonor! Woe to him who would
not be true, even though to be false were salvation.
Yea, woe to him who, as the great Pilot Paul has it,
while preaching to others is himself a castaway.*

HERMAN MELVILLE,
MOBY DICK

I don't remember anything about the show that October morning. I simply knew that my suitcase was in my trunk, and when the program was over I would drive out of those familiar gates to an unfamiliar and, to me, terrifying world.

A couple of staff members wanted to drive me to the hospital in Washington, but I was determined to go alone. I was ashamed and afraid, and I did not want anyone to see me walk through those doors.

I don't remember a lot about the good-byes except for one conversation. I had tried to slip out quietly, but one of my friends stopped me at my car. She tried to dissuade me from this journey, fearing that, in her words, "You might never be special again." I looked into her face and told her there was nothing else I could do.

The drive took about three and a half hours. I turned the radio on to an easy-listening station hoping to quiet my mind, but the words of friends and colleagues tumbled over each other.

Over and over in my mind I replayed words I'd heard in the last month:

"Do you know the damage you are doing to this ministry?"

"I always knew you would lose it someday."

"You might never be special again."

I started having serious doubts as to whether doctors would be able to help me. If I showed them a broken leg, it made sense to me that they would be able to fix that, but how do you mend a broken spirit?

I'd always thought that if I just tried hard enough, I could make everything all right. But I had failed, and look where it was taking me—to a psychiatric hospital. What would become of me there?

By the time I got to the hospital parking lot, it was dark. All I could see was the low, brick building of the psych ward that was connected to the main hospital.

It was October and very cold. I sat in my car for an hour, afraid to go in. I knew that once I walked through those doors, nothing in my life would ever be the same. I wondered how I ever ended up like this. I thought of the house I grew up in, of my brother and sister, of a simple life in a simple town that now seemed to belong to another world.

As I sat there looking for the strength to get out and walk that short distance to the hospital door, it began to rain. I prayed through my tears: "Lord, I am so afraid. I don't even know if I am doing the right thing by being here. It feels like I am running away, but I don't know where else to go. Please help me."

I got out of the car and stood for a moment watching my breath dissipate in the chill air. I opened the trunk and pulled out my suitcase. It seemed very light, and I wondered what I might have packed the night before. Lately, I was finding it hard to remember what I had done from one day to the next.

I walked up to the door and pressed the buzzer. It opened, and I walked in. A young nurse took my suitcase and asked me to sit down in the lobby for a few moments. I looked around. It was very quiet. In one corner of the room, a nurse was trying to comfort a woman who was obviously distressed. I wondered if she was a patient, or if she had just dropped off a loved one.

The nurse came back and took my blood pressure, which she said was very low. She took my temperature and then showed me to my room. It was simple and sparse, a bed, a table, a chair, and a small wardrobe. Everything was neutral and quiet. The nurse looked as if she were about my age, dressed in white: clean, clinical, safe.

"I need to go through your things. It's hospital policy," she said.

I sat on the edge of the bed and watched as she put items to one side. My hair dryer, my makeup, my belts and hose—anything I could hurt myself with. (I told her I had no intention of blow-drying myself to death!) She asked me if I needed anything, and then left for the night, telling me that someone would check on me every fifteen minutes until morning.

I sat there, numb and cold. *How is it possible that this morning I was on national television, beautifully dressed, part of a respected Christian ministry, and now I am locked up in a psychiatric ward, not even trusted with a hair dryer?*

I thought about my family. They had all been very supportive of this decision, but I wondered how it made my mother feel. Did it revive old ghosts—my father's last year in a barren hospital when he was beyond Mother's help?

I went to use the bathroom in my room and realized the door couldn't be locked. My room did not lock either. My private little world was over.

I tried to sleep, but couldn't. I wondered who had slept there before me and what had happened to them. Had their days here helped them, or were they more disabled than before?

I remembered a friend saying that when the pain of remaining the same is greater than the pain of change, you'll change. But who was to say that this would lead to anything better? When I had prayed that simple prayer of commitment to Christ as a young girl in Scotland, I never for a moment saw my life looking like this. I wanted to be a missionary to India, not a patient in a mental hospital.

I knew I was not going to be able to sleep, so I asked the night nurse if she could give me something to help. She told me she had no authorization to give medication. Her next words were both frightening and comforting: "I'm sorry that you are in so much pain, Sheila, and it will probably get worse before it gets better, but you are in a safe place."

I thought of the words of Father Marple in *Moby Dick*. I had found them quoted in a book I had read the week before. His words went over and over in my mind:

> Woe to him whom this world charms from gospel duty.
> Woe to him who seeks to pour oil upon the waters
> when God has brewed them into a gale. . . . Woe to him
> whose good name is more to him than goodness. . . .
> Yea, woe to him who, as the great Pilot Paul has it,
> while preaching to others is himself a castaway.

God had brewed my waters into a gale, and there was no calm to be found that night. In the midst of this violent upheaval I was afraid that I too would be a castaway, drowned in waters too deep for me. I knew God was there, but to what depths would he let me sink before he pulled me out? I picked up my diary and read the last entry:

> Today has been the worst day of my life. I feel so afraid
> and so alone. All my life is crumbling, and I am vulnera-
> ble and so tired. What if I can't find my way out of all this
> pain? It washes over me in great waves. I want to reach
> out to someone, but I don't know who. I feel as if I am

dying, but I am not sick. What if no one believes me? What if I become such a burden that I am simply swept aside? I am afraid that I am losing my mind. God help me.

Eventually I fell asleep—until a nurse knocked on my door at 6 A.M. I wondered for a moment where I was, and then it all came flooding back. I gazed at myself in the mirror. I looked old and tired. I had no makeup to hide behind and no desire to hide.

In search of a cup of coffee, I followed the sound of voices to the patients' lounge. The warm, familiar buzz of noise sounded inviting, but as I walked into the room, some of the patients stopped talking and stared at me. Though this was a Christian hospital, it had never even crossed my mind that I might be recognized. A man in his thirties spoke up. "Are you Sheila Walsh?"

"Yes, I am," I replied.

"The one on television?" he continued.

"Yes."

"What are you doing here?"

"I'm a patient," I said, stating the obvious.

"Yeah, right, sure you are." He laughed.

"Well, do you think I'm here to do a concert, dressed in my bathrobe?" I asked him.

One of the other patients advised him to stop talking and get me a cup of coffee, which he brought back with a large grin on his face. "Sorry, I always say too much."

The lounge looked comfortable and lived-in. Well-used chairs and a sofa were grouped around the television as if awaiting a favorite show. On the other side of the room were some small coffee tables and chairs, and a few people sat there reading or writing. I sat down on the sofa.

A young woman in a Laura Ashley robe came and sat beside me. She looked frail. She told me her name and that she was here because she had tried to take her own life. "Seems kind of wild now," she said, "but I felt so desperate, and I wanted the pain to stop."

Some of the patients went downstairs for breakfast, but because I was new, I was not allowed to leave the unit. A young man brought a tray to the lounge, and I took it to one of the coffee tables. I lifted the aluminum lid and saw two very tired eggs staring up at me. I put the lid back down.

The group gathered in a circle for the morning devotions and to check in with one another. One by one they said their names and why they were there.

"I'm Michael, and I'm here because of suicide attempts."

"I'm John, and I'm here with manic depression."

When it came to me, I didn't know what to say. "I'm Sheila, and I don't know why I am here."

A couple of people smiled at me as if they understood.

When everyone had said something, they shared prayer requests and prayed for a fruitful day for each person.

I was taken by one of the nurses for blood tests. (I gave them thirteen test tubes full!) I believed the best thing to do was to let them run every kind of test on me. I was beginning to realize some people I knew seemed glad I was having difficulty. If the rumors were true—that I suffered from manic depression, or that I was a pathological liar—then I certainly needed help. If they weren't, it would be good to have that information confirmed by a professional.

After I had given my thirteen test tubes of blood, I had my first appointment with the doctor who would be working with me. He asked me a question that seemed strange to me: "Who are you?"

I knew that there was a right answer, and yet I didn't know what it was. I told him that I was the co-host of "The 700 Club," that I was a singer, a writer, and that I knew I was floundering.

He repeated the question. "Who are you, Sheila?"

My mind went over countless photo shoots and page after page of biographical information, but I knew that this was not what he was looking for. He meant the stuff of life, the fabric of my being, but my life was what I *did*, and I didn't know what else to say.

"I don't know," I said, as tears poured down my face.

"I know that, and that is why you are here."

I thought of the morning devotional reading with the other patients:

> *The LORD is my light and my salvation—*
> *whom shall I fear?*
> *The LORD is the stronghold of my life—*
> *of whom shall I be afraid?*
>
> PSALM 27:1–2

And so began one of the greatest adventures of my life: to face the truth about myself, to face my fears, to let everything go and to trust God in the darkness.

I went out into the little courtyard reserved for patients. I sat by the stream that tumbled over the rocks and wrote in my diary:

> *When greatness seems to vanish*
> *faster than the morning mist—*
> *when purple robes dissolve beneath a touch—*
> *when crowds and cheers*
> *are hushed and stilled*
> *and spotlights turn their faces—*
> *I stand alone, I'm smiling in the dark.*
> *He who would be greatest must be the servant of all.*
> *I hear it now, a softer, truer, call.*

A softer call, "Come to me, all you who are weary and burdened, and I will give you rest" (Matthew 11:28). A truer call, "What does the LORD require of you? To act justly and to love mercy and to walk humbly with your God" (Micah 6:8).

As I sat in the quiet of the courtyard, it seemed as if the volcano had stilled for a moment. I watched a little bird sitting on the bare branch of a tree, singing a few notes to itself. The water rippled softly over the stones. In the peace of that moment, I could almost forget where I was. But I knew that the earth beneath my feet was not yet settled. Over the years, tremendous pressures had built up inside me just as the pressure that builds before a volcano. I could no longer ignore it. Vesuvius had erupted.

Of course, I'll never fail you.
You can count on me.
I'm the one who is always faithful.
I feel my feet are slipping.
I hear them count me out.
I'm lost, faithless. I'll never make it home.

3

Hiding in the Shadows

We shall not cease from exploration
And the end of all our exploring
Will be to arrive where we started
And know the place for the first time.
T. S. ELIOT, *"LITTLE GIDDING"*

I slipped easily into the regimented routine of the hospital. Out of bed at 6 A.M., breakfast, devotions, individual therapy, and group therapy. After lunch, an art class or more psychological testing and evaluation. The evenings were usually free to watch television or work out in the gym.

Early in my hospital stay, I was concerned about my own well-being. What's more, I was concerned about what would happen to people who had been in a crisis and who had listened to me on television, people who had prayed with me and made a commitment to change. Would they now throw away any good that had been done, believing that nothing of lasting value could flow through a broken vessel? I was sure that some of the people who had placed me on a very high pedestal were truly devastated when that pedestal began to crumble.

I talked to my doctor about this issue for days. He asked me who I had been holding up as the answer: Sheila Walsh or Jesus Christ? I knew what he was getting at, and I knew that Jesus is the only enduring hope for any of us. But

I also knew that privilege brings responsibility. We are called to live in a way that honors God. Somewhere along the road, however, I had crossed the line between pointing to the One who is the answer, and feeling an overwhelming burden to show what that can look like here on earth.

For ten years I had traveled all over the world, singing and speaking. When I thought back on the things I had talked about onstage, they were the things I knew God in his goodness wants for us all; they were the things I wanted in my own life. So when someone would ask me to pray for her marriage, I did it with all my heart, knowing that God would be delighted to hear the prayer. If someone wanted prayer to find peace in his life, I gladly prayed with passion that this gift of God would be granted.

Gradually, my life onstage became more real to me than my life offstage. When I began to feel that my life was crumbling, I talked more. I talked louder. I tried to talk what-was-not into being, as if the very act of calling it out would make it a reality for me too.

In the hospital I received mail from people who knew I had been admitted. They called me a hypocrite. One person sent tapes of talks I had given and copies of articles I had written that seemed ridiculous in light of where I now was. I had spoken so much and so loudly that my own words came back to mock me. Each mail delivery felt like one more nail in my coffin.

It was as if I had taken my two favorite children's stories and lived one, while longing for the other.

THE WIZARD'S WORLD

I have always loved the story *The Wizard of Oz*. As a child, I was enchanted when Dorothy's world changed from black-and-white to color. Like all children, I adored the Scarecrow and the Cowardly Lion and the Tin Man, and I wanted my very own Toto. (I also thought that the witch looked suspiciously like the woman who served our school meals and made me eat brussels sprouts!)

Years later, I saw myself not as Dorothy, but as the little man behind the curtain, who, when the truth was revealed, was no wizard at all. When Dorothy discovers that instead of being a ferocious, larger-than-life wizard, he is just a man, she tells him, "You are a very bad man." To this, he replies, "No, my dear, I am just a very bad wizard."

That is how I felt in the hospital; I felt like a very bad wizard.

If the wizard in the story had lived without the bells and whistles, he could have simply told people that they would find what they were looking for as they continued on their journeys. That is what actually happened anyway. But no one wanted to wait that long. They wanted a miracle right then.

Like the wizard, I wanted to be able to make everything better for everyone, hoping that the edges of other people's miracles would touch me.

It must have been a huge relief to the wizard when the grand charade was over. The "bad wizard" was actually a very nice man! I felt relief too. It was painful but liberating to have the curtain pulled away. All I wanted now was to be one of the people on the journey.

Something about television makes you larger than life, particularly Christian television. Whenever I would bump into viewers in a shopping mall or grocery store, it seemed to me that they believed I had a hot line to heaven, a number that God would pick up before he answered calls from "mere mortals." I'm sure part of it was simply that I was recognizable as a Christian; they knew they could ask me to pray for them. But at times it spilled over into something that scared me.

I remember a man who drove with his very sick wife for ten hours to visit me because he believed that she would be healed if I would pray for her. It was a privilege to pray for this woman, but why did he have to drive so far when God was with them all along?

I talked with him about that, and his answer was that God was more likely to listen to me. Because he had made too many mistakes in his life, he wasn't worthy of an answer. When he looked at me on his television screen, he saw someone with the key to the executive washroom. I tried to explain that none of us deserves an answer, that it is all God's grace, but I don't think he believed me. To him, it sounded too good to be true.

How ironic. It's as if we have taken the truth and made it a fairy tale, and taken a fairy tale and made it the truth. Life would be so much easier if all we had to do was to find our way down that yellow brick road to God, and there in the Emerald City he would grant our every wish. We would bring our fear and our anger and our pain and our sickness to him, and with a puff of smoke and a thundering voice he would take them all away. There would be no obstacles on the road, no enemies determined to stop us from completing our journey—just a clear, golden path.

The truth is that there *will* be a day when all sorrow and suffering will be dispelled and every tear wiped away. That is a promise, but it is a promise of a day to come. How shall we live till then?

That is where my other favorite childhood story comes in.

LOVED TO LIFE

Now this is a glorious story!

If you have never read *The Velveteen Rabbit*, please buy a copy. It is truly a gift. To me, it is a parable of biblical import. When the story begins, the cloth Rabbit is plush and new, stuffed inside a little boy's Christmas stocking. Other new toys come along, ones that *do* things, ones that make noises, and somehow the little Rabbit gets lost in the shuffle.

In the quiet of the night, the toys talk to one another. One toy, the old Skin Horse, is consistently kind to the Rabbit. One day the Rabbit asks him, "What is Real?"

"Real isn't how you are made," said the Skin Horse. "It's a thing that happens to you, when a child loves you for a long time."

The Rabbit asks the Skin Horse if it hurts to become real. The Skin Horse, who is always truthful, says that it does sometimes, but when you are real, you don't mind being hurt. He tells the little Rabbit that becoming real does not generally happen to those who have to be carefully kept. That's because by the time that you are real, most of your fur has been loved off. I identify with the Rabbit's sigh; if only we could become real without it hurting, without it taking so much time.

The Skin Horse had the wisdom that is born out of time to those who listen to their lives. He had watched all the trends that come and go, but he knew there is no eternity in fashion. When new, he himself had been loved by a little boy, and the marks of that love were etched on the furless patches of his body, his tail hair pulled out to string beads.

Unlike the wizard, the Skin Horse had no bells and whistles, just a calm surrender to the process of life, a deep awareness of what real love looks like. He had spent himself on his master, with no thought for himself, believing this was what he was made for. His shoes were old and worn, but they fit like a glove.

Not so for the wizard. The wizard was meeting a need, but he was living a lie. When the curtain fell back, it revealed a little old man sweating, huffing and puffing to maintain the facade. He looked as if he were about to have a heart attack. There was nothing comfortable or natural about his life. The old Skin Horse was far from being the latest thing in the nursery, but he was loved for who he really was. As he said, "When you are Real, you can never be ugly except to people who don't understand."

The message of those two stories was clear to me. I could spend the rest of my life behind the drapes, pulling levers and talking loudly, or I could find out what I was really made for. I wanted so badly to be real. It is one thing to find stories that shed a little light on our paths, but how do we live in the midst of our own stories when it seems as if no good can come of any of it?

After a few days in the hospital, it became clear to me that the Lord had been trying to get my attention for a long time. Books I had read in preparation for my show rang distant bells in my mind. I would read certain pages over and over as I compiled a list of questions for my guests, sensing there was something I needed to understand, but I could never quite grasp hold of what it was.

Now I was in a place where I had the luxury of time. Here I could begin to look at my life.

It had been a pattern of mine in the past to suppress uncomfortable feelings. I didn't know what else to do with them. So when I was unable or unwilling to deal with what was true about my life, I buried it. Even though I ended up walking on a lumpy carpet, it had begun to feel normal.

> *Denial is my closest friend—*
> *it keeps the world at bay;*
> *it makes me dance to any tune*
> *and say what I should say;*
> *it builds a wall around my heart*
> *invisible but strong.*
> *I'm always there*
> *but never quite belong.*

I watched as others at the clinic began to have the courage to deal with things they hated about their lives. One of the women lost control one morning in a group session and threw her chair across the room. (She had seemed like such a nice, quiet person!) When she finally gained enough control to talk, we discovered that she had been brutally raped as a young girl and had never told anyone. Instead, she had thrown herself into Christian ministry to try and numb the pain.

The group talked together for a long time. The woman felt that somehow the rape was her fault, and she needed to restore the balance in her life; she must have done something to cause this rape, and she needed to pay for it. She had discovered that if she worked punishingly hard every day, she didn't have to deal with the anger boiling just below the surface. She believed that if her anger ever escaped, it would consume her. She was sure that if anyone in the Christian organization where she worked found out what had happened to her, they would ask her to leave. To avoid being found out, she had chosen to live in the shadows. What I saw powerfully enacted before me that day is this: You can try for years to deny the things that are tearing at your soul, but they will not go away. They thrive in the shadowlands.

NO SHADOWLANDS WITH CHRIST

At the request of a counselor, I began to study the way that Jesus lived among his friends and the way he lived among the people whose paths he crossed. I took a long look at two different people who were in trouble: a woman who knew her life was in chaos, and a man who had no idea what he would become when the pressure of life became intense.

The woman's story is found in John 4:1–42. The first miracle was that Jesus talked to this Samaritan woman at all, for Jews had nothing to do with Samaritans. Not only did Christ talk to this woman, but he also asked her for a drink, which would have been unheard of in those times.

This woman knew she was in trouble. I would imagine the distant rumble had become a very familiar sound to her, as it had for me. Relationally, her life was a mess. She had been married five times and was now living with a man who was not her husband. I doubt she had many friends. She would have been mistrusted by women and joked about among men.

But Jesus looked at her—really looked at her—and talked to her as if she mattered, because to him, she did. Something about that gaze connected with her, because the woman came clean with him. She had no need to step out of her shadows into the sunlight for a stranger, but she revealed to Jesus that the man she was living with was not her husband. What a gift Christ gave her in letting her know that he was aware of this and of all the rest as well. If he had offered her living water without ever revealing that he knew all the truth about her, perhaps she would have let his words of life bypass her, thinking, *If you only knew.* But he loved her enough to let her know, "I know it all, and I still love you." That unfamiliar and glorious gift changed her life so that, even as she was gulping it down, she was running to tell others the Good News.

"I know it all, and I still love you." That is the convicting, convincing, liberating truth that comes from an encounter with Christ: All is known; there is no need to pretend anymore. I wrestled with that truth, but it is hard to lay aside a mask when it looks so like you, and you have worn it for so long that you can't remember what you look like without it.

I imagine the Samaritan was a changed woman after that day. We don't hear any more of her story, but after encountering Jesus, she was fully known and fully loved for the first time in her life. She had looked into the face of God, and he was smiling.

The Skin Horse was content with his bruised and battered exterior because his fur had been loved off by someone who treasured him. The nameless woman whom Jesus met at the well was scarred and bruised too, but her wounds were in her spirit. Not until she came face-to-face with Christ did she catch a glimpse of what she was really made for. She knew she was in trouble—no one had to convince her of that—and when Jesus confronted her with who she was and then offered her a better way to live, she grasped hold of it with every fiber of her being.

It is much more difficult to deal with the truth about your life when you have no idea that you have feet of clay and it suddenly begins to rain. That's what happened with another gospel character, Jesus' friend Simon Peter.

Peter was a rough, strong, loud, salt-of-the-earth fisherman, the kind of friend you would lean on in a crisis. He was passionately committed to following Christ, wherever that took him. When Jesus began to talk of a different end to his life than the one Peter had imagined, Peter was confused and hurt. He could never imagine leaving Jesus, let alone deny knowing him. Surely their relationship had come too far for that. And yet one night Jesus said Peter would deny him before morning. In anguish Peter cried out that he would die before letting that happen.

I saw so much of myself in this man: bold and utterly confident in his own abilities to overcome any obstacle in his way. He *knew* Jesus could count on him. Christ gave Peter a glimpse into the horror that lay just around the corner and let him know that, when it was all over, not only would Jesus still love Peter, but he also had a job for him to do: "When you have turned back, strengthen your brothers" (Luke 22:32).

I wonder how Peter must have felt the day Jesus was executed for crimes he did not commit. Can you begin to grasp the horror of knowing that, when it counted the most, you were not there for your friend—your Lord?

When I used to read that passage, I didn't see myself in Peter's place. It was very familiar to me as part of the passion story, but I had no real empathy for Peter as a man who had to choke on his own words—until mine came back to mock me. Peter, who with his own lips had denied ever knowing Jesus, just as Jesus said he would. Luke tells us that Peter "went outside and wept bitterly" (22:62). There was no comforting Peter that night. What could his wife say to him? How could anyone take that pain away? When Christ had needed him most, he had been the one to drive the first nail in. Bitter night turned to morning, another endless day; then the darkness closed in on him again.

It was the first day of a new week when Mary came running down the road, screaming to Peter: "His body is gone. Someone has taken him. The tomb is empty." As words tumbled over words, Peter was already out the door. It was true. The grave had been robbed, and the body was gone. Later that night, as the disciples cowered in a locked room, out of control, afraid for their own lives, Jesus came and stood among them and said, "Peace be with you!"

They had thought they would never hear his voice again. Peter had thought he would never hear the word *peace* again. But how could he look Jesus in the eye? After all, Jesus had known that Peter would fail him, and he had.

But history records that, for Peter, life was not over yet. John 21 tells the following story: One morning more than a week later, the fishermen disciples met Jesus for the third time since his resurrection; he sat with them on the beach, cooking breakfast. When they had finished eating, Jesus turned and looked at Peter. "Simon son of John, do you truly love me more than these?"

When Peter said yes, he did, Jesus asked him the question again.

Peter again said, "Yes, Lord, you know that I love you."

Jesus asked for a third time and this, to me, is one of the most honest, confrontational, liberating dialogues recorded anywhere. Peter looked at Jesus, I would imagine with deep pain in his eyes, and said to him, "Lord, you know all things; you know that I love you."

Peter was really saying, *You knew that I would fail you, even when I talked louder than anyone else. You knew that I am not as strong as I thought I was. So if you knew all that, Lord, you know my heart is broken now, and you know that I love you.*

Peter was given a second chance. He went on to become a martyr of the early church, and as the early church father Tertullian wrote, "the blood of the martyrs is seed." Peter's life and death fed the church, for from that life-changing confrontation with Christ on the beach, he was a different man, a man who selflessly gave himself to the building up of the body of Christ. "You are Peter, and upon this rock I will build my church" (Matthew 16:18).

> *"O God, I am only dust," I cry*
> *and God picks up the dust*
> *and breathes his life once more.*

Sometimes I think we misinterpret faith. In my own life, instead of grabbing hold of what was wrong with it and dealing with it, no matter how painful it was, I acted as if everything were fine. I thought if I just *believed* enough, then everything would be all right. But was I living by faith or by wishful thinking? Jesus never encouraged his friends to cover over the pain in their lives but to bring it into the light, where healing is found. Sometimes we don't do that, because we fear being rejected by others. Yes, rejection may well happen, but bringing the pain to the light is still the best way to live.

Sometimes we simply don't want to face the truth about ourselves; the myth reads so much better. Sometimes we do not seek help because it will mean we have to change, and change is painful and unpredictable. To me, now, faith is bringing all that is true about our lives into the blinding light of God's grace. It is believing that he will still be there at the end of the journey. And so will we, perhaps a little bloodied, probably with a limp and possibly, as the Skin Horse said, with most of our hair loved off, but we will be there.

JUST AS I AM

On the second Sunday I was in the hospital, I had permission to go to church with a nurse. I let the singing of those glorious hymns wash over me as we sat in the back row. The pastor spoke about those of us who feel we have failed God in our mission on this earth. I looked at the nurse out of the corner of my eye, wondering if she had had a word with him before the service, but in my heart I knew it was the Lord. (That is just like him!) I felt as if God's presence had invaded every corner of the sanctuary. I couldn't lift my head. It was as if I were on holy ground.

The pastor concluded the sermon with an illustration. "There are some of you here today who feel like dead people. It is as if you are already six feet under, staring up at the top of your own locked coffin. This morning, Jesus wants to set you free. You simply have to let go of the key and pass it through the little hole, where you see a tiny shaft of light."

I listened as if I were the only person in the room. He was speaking to me. This was exactly how I felt. I had never gone forward to an altar before; I had prayed to be accepted into God's family in my bedroom. I asked the nurse if it would be all right if I spent a few moments at the altar, and she said yes. As I walked the aisle that day, I did not care who saw me or what they thought. All I knew was that I was dying and someone was telling me where to get help.

I knelt at the altar with my head on my hands and tears coursing through my fingers. All I could say was, "Lord, forgive me. I am sorry that I have lived a lie for so long, pretending to be fine but being miserable inside, trying to talk things into being, too afraid to deal with what was wrong in my own home for fear it would consume me. And now a lot of people will be hurt by the fallout. I am so sorry. I can't make it right. I give it all over to you. Show me what to do."

When Christ confronted me with the truth about my life, his words were the strongest and yet the most loving I would hear. They would help me through the next part of the journey.

> *Gracious Father,*
> *you know us so well.*
> *You love us so completely.*
> *Forgive us, we pray,*
> *for hiding in the shadows.*
> *Give us the courage to live in the light,*
> *for you are Light,*
> *and you are Truth,*
> *and we are your children.*
> *Amen.*

A winter landscape
no relief
a cold gray blanket
settles on my soul.

4

Winter

I am in that temper that if I were under water
I would scarcely kick to come to the top.
JOHN KEATS

Scotland is known for its beautiful scenery. When the
sun shines, there is no better place to be on this earth. The
trouble is that it does not shine very often! On the west coast
of Scotland, where my family lives, there are a lot of what we
call drizzly days. On drizzly days, the sky is gray and heavy, the
wind is bitingly cold, and it's not really raining, it's drizzling.
The weather on days like these is like a cold, damp blanket
wrapped around your shoulders. People hurry home from
town, from church, eager to throw off their raincoats and
boots and gather by a roaring fire, where the misery of the elements can be consumed by the crackling flames.

I liked winter in Scotland. It was quiet, and the sea could
finally be heard, since the tourists had gone home. I would
come home from school, take off my navy and gold blazer,
pull on some jeans and a warm sweater, and head down to the
ocean. I would sit there for a long time, enjoying the songs of
the sea. Sometimes I would settle onto a rock, close enough
to get splashed by the salty spray. I loved it. That was where
I did my serious praying. Out there, surrounded by the wind

and the water, I knew I served an awesome God. This was no sideshow; this was a tiny glimpse of the splendor of the Lord of heaven and earth. Those winter days are part of who I am—a winter person. I love the reds and the yellows of the world, the brighter side, but there will always be a place in my heart for the grays and ebony shades of life.

But what happened to me in the summer of '92 was different from that gentle melancholy. There was nothing comforting or familiar about any of it. A volcano is a splendid sight, but when it is over, everything around it is desolate, covered in white ash—a silent, winter landscape.

In the spring of that year I had visited a counselor. I felt sad most of the time, and I didn't know why. I just knew I was very tired. It was as though winter had settled on my heart with no hope of spring. One of our camera operators said to me one day that I seemed depressed, but I did not really know what that meant. I remembered years before when I was touring in England, the same subject had come up. I was on the road with another artist, and a few of us sat down one evening after the concert to eat. Someone said, "Did you hear about Dave?"

A few snippets of information were tossed into the arena, and then someone said, "He has been diagnosed with clinical depression."

The general response of the crowd was complete disbelief, and the jokes began to circulate around the table. I know that we British tend to be a little caustic in our wit, but the general consensus of opinion was that there is no such thing as depression.

"He just needs to pull himself together, that's all."

"We all have bad days; you just can't give in to them."

"I've always thought he was a bit lazy."

I remember arguing with them because I knew this man and it made no sense to me that he would be pretending to be in so much pain. But the subject soon changed, and

I didn't give it much more thought. All that I knew was that my friend was sad, and I understood that.

I would eventually come to understand a lot more about depression.

> *Nothing is what it seems.*
> *I reach for you but you are not there.*
> *I cry for help and you are all around,*
> *keeping me contained*
> *safe and cold within a Hall of Mirrors.*
> *I tell myself that this is the real world,*
> *but my head aches*
> *and my heart aches*
> *and I know this is a lie.*

If you are on a speeding train that is out of control, and you know that you are losing your hold, what do you do? Do you wait till it hits the wall, or do you jump off? I decided to jump. I knew I would be hurt, but I didn't care anymore. I had let things get to a place where I could no longer function.

Statistics tell us that more than thirty million Americans are affected by depression. One of the greatest challenges to those who suffer with this disease is that many people do not believe it is a legitimate illness. I can assure you, it is.

After a couple of days of medical tests in the hospital, I met with the chief psychiatrist to review the results and find out what was wrong with me. He seemed a kind man, with an easy manner and a strong sense of humor, which I imagine serves him well in his chosen profession. He told me he saw no signs of manic depression but that I was severely clinically depressed. I exhibited classic signs of clinical depression: an inability to sleep (I woke up between three and four o'clock every morning), loss of appetite, overwhelming feelings of hopelessness, loss of memory, inability to concentrate, loss of emotional control, acute anxiety, and an enduring, unbearable sadness.

The doctor explained more about clinical depression. Clinical depression has many contributing factors, some of which can be physiological. Within the brain there are chemical messengers called neurotransmitters. When these neurotransmitters are at a healthy, normal level, we are able to function well. But the lack of one or more of three chemical transmitters—serotonin, norepinephrine, and dopamine—can be a key contributor to depression. He continued to say my brain needed help in replacing those levels, which were very low. He advised my taking a drug called Zoloft for a while.

I was resistant to the idea of medication for three reasons. First, as a Christian dealing with an emotional and mental crisis, I was skeptical about the wisdom of resorting to pills. Surely I could get through this crisis without them. The cumulative words of so many of our guests on "The 700 Club" came back to me: "If I had enough faith, would I be in this place at all?"

Second, I also believed that God was asking me to look at my life and take responsibility for where I found myself. I believed I needed to feel whatever pain was necessary in order to finally come to grips with my life. I did not want a "feel good" pill to dull the edges.

My third concern was the fear that I would be walking around with a vacant look in my eyes and drool on my bathrobe, weaving a basket and being followed by my imaginary dog, with whom I would be carrying on a constant dialogue! If there was any chance of this happening, I wanted no part of a drug treatment.

My doctor alleviated my fears. Zoloft, he said, is what they call a serotonin uptake inhibitor, which would slow down the rate at which my body was using up that valuable messenger. Though it does not solve underlying issues that need to be dealt with, it does give a physical boost—when you see the possibility of spring, you have more strength to walk through the weeks till its arrival.

I went ahead and took the prescription and within a few days I could already tell a difference. Rather than numb me to the things that I needed to deal with, it helped me regain my balance and made me better able to face the long road ahead. Each morning, as I lined up with my fellow patients, I took that little blue pill with a prayer of thanksgiving.

AMONG FRIENDS

Many of my new friends whose diagnosis was the same as mine were highly motivated, disciplined people—doctors, pastors, students—who, like me, in the midst of their apparent success, felt the walls were closing in on them. Each of us could have echoed the words of Abraham Lincoln when he said,

> I am now the most miserable man living. If what I feel were equally distributed to the whole human family, there would not be one cheerful face on earth. Whether I shall ever be better I cannot tell. I awfully forebode that I shall not. To remain as I am is impossible, I must die or be better, it appears to me.

Lincoln struggled with depression for most of his adult life. I wonder if anyone understood what was happening to him and stood beside him, or did he have to walk alone? In the midst of this gray, winter landscape one thing was clear to me: I was not alone. There was a nail-scarred figure walking with me through the snow.

> *When I said, "My foot is slipping,"*
> *your love, O LORD, supported me.*
> *When anxiety was great within me,*
> *your consolation brought joy to my soul.*
> PSALM 94:18–19

In the hospital, God gave me—and other patients—clear signs that we were not suffering in solitude. One encounter I will never forget. I had been there for a couple of weeks and felt pretty much at home. After dinner one evening, I was wandering through the lobby to go to my room, when I became aware of a family approaching the front door. Two daughters were supporting their mother, who was crying and moaning as she got closer to the front door.

I recognized that look, so I decided to hang around and give this sad older woman a hug as she came in. Then the strangest thing happened. The mother looked up at me, let out a cry, and threw her arms around me. When the daughters saw the scene, they too began to cry.

I was a little bemused. I wanted to be welcoming, but I was exceeding my own expectations! Eventually, one of the daughters pulled herself together enough to tell me what was happening. This lovely woman had lived for forty years with a man who brutally beat her. Her children had tried to persuade her to leave him many times, but as a Christian she wanted to honor the vows she had made to God all those years ago. She had finally left after one terrible beating, but was so overwhelmed with guilt and fear that she had settled into a deep depression. Her daughters were very concerned about her and had spent a long time trying to persuade her to get some help. They could see she was sinking fast, but she was very afraid and ashamed of being admitted to a psychiatric hospital.

As they drove to D.C., they prayed that the Lord would give her a sign as she walked through the door—a sign that she was in a safe place. That's where I came in. She had watched me on television every day and saw me as another daughter. When I was there at the door, she—and her daughters—saw me as the "sign." Isn't that just like the Lord? He cared for this dear woman so much that he placed us there together, at just the right moment.

WEEPING WITH THOSE WHO WEEP

One of the questions I continue to wrestle with is "What is real faith?" I believe it will always be God's will to restore families, to mend broken lives so that we can continue to walk together. I hold that truth close to my heart as I walk in a broken, fallen world. What I think we as the church lack, though, is a place to talk about how things really are now. In our desire to be an inspiration to one another we often veil what is true, because what is true is not always inspirational. But hurting believers whose lives are in tatters often need real help. If we were able to put aside our need for approval long enough to be authentic, then, surely, we would be living as the church.

Sometimes we encourage one another to live inauthentic lives. My mother once told me a story of an experience she had when she was dating my father. They twice visited a new church that placed great emphasis on praising God in the midst of trials. This is obviously a scriptural mandate, so who could fault them? At one particular meeting, a young woman who had just lost a baby stood up and gave thanks for the trials in her life, giving glory to the Lord, that in him there is no need to grieve; we can continue to march on victoriously. My mother was horrified by this woman's apparent indifference to the loss of her child, but the rest of the congregation clapped in approval. After the service ended, my mom heard someone in the bathroom weeping bitterly in one of the cubicles. It was the mother who, having done the *right thing*, was now expressing her genuine emotions all alone in a dark place.

It makes me so angry to think that someone in such terrible pain had to weep alone. Perhaps you think this story sounds extreme, but versions of it are played out every day in our evangelical communities. We all experience loss at some point in our lives, whether it be the loss of a marriage, a career, a loved one, or a dream, and too often we are disapproved of by others who are insensitive to our pain.

I remember when the movie *Field of Dreams* opened. I was living in Los Angeles at the time and went to see it in one of those huge theaters that seats about fifteen hundred people. The story concerned a man who had given up on his childhood dreams for his life and now felt that it was too late to reclaim them. He wore his disillusionment like a heavy chain around his ankle everywhere he went. In the movie, he is given a second chance to do what he had always dreamed of—to play with the baseball greats. I am an avid people watcher, and what I saw that night surprised me. At the end of the movie I saw men file past me, heads down. I could tell that some of them had been crying. I assume they had identified with having a lost dream and hoping it still might someday be fulfilled.

I thought about that movie for a long time. I came to the conclusion that many of us lose our way to some extent. We compromise a little here and there, let go of something we treasure for something that we are told is worth more, and sometimes lose touch with the life we imagined we would live. Part of that is inevitable in the process of aging, but I believe we need to acknowledge losses and grieve their passing. Too many of us are embarrassed by grief. We don't know what to say to one another, so we distance ourselves and say nothing. Society moves so quickly that we act as if we only need a few Cliff notes to deal with any number of crises.

I remember a colleague who was diagnosed with cancer. He was married, with children who needed their daddy around. People made plans to bring this man in to work one day so that we could all gather around him and pray for his healing. After we had finished, the man leading the prayer time said, "Go and walk in your healing." I'm not quite sure what that meant, but there seemed to be a general consensus that everything was all right now.

Several months later, the man died. It seemed to me that we got his funeral over with pretty quickly and moved on. We didn't talk about it. There seemed to be no accountability to our words at all, just a faint embarrassment and the unspoken indictment that there must have been something else about the man we did not know. Perhaps he harbored some unconfessed resentment in his heart, or a sin of the past was still tied round his leg like a millstone. When I think back to that time and the way that we all handled it, the man who died seemed to be the only one who was not afraid.

HONESTLY

When we don't deal honestly with our lives and the losses we face, when we try to anesthetize the pain and move on, then the suppressed anger or fear or guilt will deal with us until we are ready to deal with those issues.

When the Israelites were carried off into captivity in Babylon, Psalm 137 says they sat down by the river and wept. Jeremiah records the despondency that lay upon the people as they remembered their homeland. They had lost their homes; they had lost their joy. God was still on the throne but his people were in pain, and they wept that pain out. I wonder sometimes if we think it ungodly to mourn the changing seasons of life, as if doing so were to question God's wisdom. I do not believe that expressing the pain we feel diminishes God or our faith in him. Everything in our lives comes to us through the gracious hands of the Lord, but that does not mean our lives will be free of pain. In fact, we are told that life will include hurt and hard times.

> *A time to kill and a time to heal,*
> *a time to tear down and a time to build,*
> *a time to weep and a time to laugh,*
> *a time to mourn and a time to dance.*
>
> ECCLESIASTES 3:3–4

If we do not tear down, we can never lastingly build. If we do not take time to mourn, we will have no joy in dancing, and if we do not fall down on our faces at times and weep, we will never be swept away with laughter. Jesus said: "Blessed are you who weep now, for you will laugh" (Luke 6:21). Ironically, we seem to have a love affair with the lighter side of life, as if any intensity of emotion would consume us.

Perhaps too, in the "shift-the-blame" society we live in, we have forgotten how to weep over our sins. David, the psalm writer, said, "When I kept silent, my bones wasted away through my groaning all day long" (Psalm 32:3). I wonder if so many of us rush off to self-help groups because we have lost the ability to be real in our churches.

Lately, many articles written in fundamentalist circles have warned against seeking psychological and psychiatric help, describing them as tools of Satan. It is true that among the tidal wave of pop psychology and self-help manuals there have been many that have served to further debilitate, but someone who is ill does need help. I have no time for programs that encourage us to pass the blame to others, but it is my experience that there *can* be tremendous value in taking a long hard look at our lives, understanding some of the reasons we made the choices we made, making peace with the past and moving beyond the past, beyond the winter to spring.

I now think it takes more faith to name our need than to keep *believing* that something will happen and not doing anything about it. It takes faith to get help, to take the first painful step toward the dream that is in our hearts. I have stood before crowds and delivered passionate messages on what I was believing was possible in my own personal life, but I know now that you can look at bricks and cement for years, believing in the vision of a home, but until you get down on your hands and knees and start to build, it will remain a dream.

There is today still an incredible stigma attached to any illness of the mind. Countless people have told me that they suffered silently for years, afraid to tell anyone how they were feeling. No intelligent person would condemn someone for having a brain tumor, so why do many people discount or distance themselves from a different form of trouble? What is, is. Depression will not go away by pretending that it does not exist.

While I was in the hospital, I was very shaken when a couple of people telephoned one evening and encouraged me to leave; they believed that a Christian shouldn't be in a "place like that." I have heard various other attempts—some that seem contradictory to others—to rationalize depression in the church:

"It is a punishment from God."

"To seek help is to doubt God's ability to heal."

"If we suffer enough, God will be pleased."

"It is a spiritual illness that should only be treated by God's personal intervention."

PERMISSION TO GET HELP

My doctor encouraged me to face the truth about my life: to stop running, stop making excuses, to step up to the plate and take responsibility for my own life.

We all need to come to a point when we will take responsibility for our choices and our healing. If you are struggling on alone, sinking a little more every day, I would encourage you to get help. Depression is a treatable illness, and there is no shame in reaching out for help.

But depression is also only one of the ways we are alerted to trouble inside of us. Some people drink to forget; this, and other addictions, treat the surface problem but they don't make the underlying problem go away. Other people are alerted by a general disquiet in their souls, a haunting rumble that says all is not well. If the trouble is in a marriage, too often people wait to get help only when both partners are "ready." While this is obviously the ideal scenario, it may not happen that way. You can choose health for only one person: yourself. Yet so often people wait and wait as their lives crumble a little more every day. It takes courage to ask for help, but only by asking will we find the help we need.

I know that those daughters I met in the hospital would have given anything to encourage their mother to seek help

61

sooner, but once she finally did it they stood by her every day and spoke what was true to her, no matter how heartbreaking the truth was.

One day we will all stand alone and answer to God for the choices we have made in our lives. It will not be enough to say we did not get help because no one would come with us. Life is not easy, but we make it much more difficult when we refuse to be honest about what we feel. For the short-term, not being honest may seem easier, but in the long haul, we pay a heavy price.

When I decided to get some help with my life, I had no idea where that path would take me. All I knew and held onto daily was that Jesus loved me. As we began to uncover some painful issues, I felt as if my heart was being ripped out of my body, but I still knew that Jesus loved me. We have this fact to hold onto in the darkest nights of our lives. It will never change. It will always be true. Yes, Jesus loves me!

Most often, what holds us back from being honest is fear. I have discovered that glass cages may look nice, but they are no place to live.

> One day I decide to see if there is more
> beyond these mocking, mirrored walls;
> there is only one way out:
> It is through the glass.
> I cut my hands, my feet, my heart.
> I think I'll bleed to death,
> but the ground I am on is solid,
> though covered with my blood.
> I look over my shoulder
> to see my glassy cage,
> but it's not there.
> It was only an illusion,
> an illusion strong enough to make me bleed.

If you are struggling to try and help someone who is dealing with depression, don't worry about saying the right thing, just *be there*. The ministry of presence is a beautiful gift to take to a sickbed. There is also something so healing about touch. Scripture illustrates the power of the laying on of hands.

I know it can be difficult to deal with something that seems to take so long to lift. Winter is a cold, harsh season that offers little comfort or shelter. It is a bleak and weary landscape, but underneath that heavy blanket, there is life, new life; it just takes time. As I understand God's Word, it is not the pace of the race that matters, but that we all finish together. It's like a story a friend once told me.

He was watching the Special Olympics on television. During the course of one of the races, a Down's syndrome boy fell facedown onto the track. There was a gasp from the crowd as they watched the boy's dreams being dashed on the merciless tarmac. Suddenly all the other runners stopped, went back, and picked him up, and they crossed the finish line together. We have much to learn from the so-called disabled.

There are many people in the church who live under the weight of depression as if it were a broken arm that may well heal if left alone. But "leaving it alone" is not the solution. I discovered that depression was not the core of my problem. Although it is a very real illness that needs to be treated, clinical depression, unlike manic depression, is usually brought on by external and internal stressors. It is the rumblings *inside* the volcano that cause the eruption. For me, depression was the flag that was trying to get my attention. I would be shocked by what it showed me.

Lord, it is dark.
I can't see the path ahead of me.
You are the light of the world,
and so I ask that you would show me the way.
I have trusted you in the daylight.
I trust you now in the night.
Amen.

Part 2

The Valley

꩜

Today I am afraid.
My enemies are many;
they march up to my door
and blow with all their might.
They take my name and tar and feather it
for all the world to see.
I stand and watch.
They whisper in my ear,
"It's all over.
The curtain's coming down.
The crowd is going home.
The lights are going out."

꩜

5

Why Are You Afraid?

*To live with fear and not be afraid
is the final test of maturity.*
EDWARD WEEKS,
BETTER THAN GOLD

Imagine with me for a moment overhearing a dialogue occurring in the throne room of heaven. The subject of the debate is how to answer Sheila Walsh's prayer.

"She says she is tired of being afraid. Perhaps we could give her the gift of courage?"

"It might be a finer gift to remove all the things that she is afraid of."

"We could always bring her home if it becomes too much for her."

A strong, quiet voice speaks up, "No. We will invite her greatest fears to visit her. They will take up residence for a while. It is only in living with them that she will ever overcome them."

That is how it seemed to me. It was as if everything I have ever been afraid of decided to take center stage in my life.

Fear felt like a physical illness to me. It was as though it had a stranglehold on my heart and mind. It made me literally, physically sick. It is one thing to be afraid of the school bully or to have nightmares as a child or to hate the dark, but it is another thing when we carry those fears into our adult lives and allow them to dictate how we should live.

THE TESTS REVEAL ...

Let me take you back to my first morning in the hospital. After they had taken my blood, I went through hours of psychological testing. I was extremely tired and found it hard to think, but perhaps that was the best scenario because I couldn't work out what would be the right answer; I could only say what came to my mind. The doctor held up pictures and asked me to tell the story behind the scene. I answered question after question till my head ached. Finally, at eight o'clock at night, the testing was finished.

A few days later that same doctor called me into his office to discuss the results. "The tests indicate that you are very angry and sad inside, Sheila, but you never give yourself permission to feel the anger or to speak up for yourself. You need people to approve of you. You allow fear to make many of your choices. It is as if there is a huge empty place inside of you, but you don't let anyone in. How does that sound to you?"

I started to smile. I'd been there less than a week, but it had already become a joke among the other patients that I did everything right. I was even the first in line every morning to get my medication!

Actually, his words made me sad because they rang so true. Fear, anger, need for approval, loneliness—all were deeply rooted in me, and I would soon come to see that they were all closely connected and major factors in my depression.

The doctor asked me what I was so afraid of.

I gave him one answer: I was afraid of losing what defined me; I was afraid that if you took away all the fancy wrapping of my life and looked inside the box, it would be empty.

But that answer led to others. I was very afraid of certain types of people, not because I wanted to win their approval, but because I believed they could wipe me away if they decided to. If I had to deal with a man with a driven personality who was easily angered, for instance, I would dance around him mentally, taking his temperature to make sure he would not blow. I couldn't see that someone could be very angry with me and say what was on his mind without destroying me in the process. At the deepest level, I feared for my survival. My life was like a tightrope, where balance is everything, and if you lose concentration for even a moment, all will be lost.

I was also afraid of anger itself. I remember when I was about twenty years old, spending a day in Glasgow with my brother. We were walking down one of the busiest streets in the city, when a man came up to Stephen and gave him a pen. It was a very basic con, the principle being that once you actually have the pen in your hand, you "owe" the man some money.

My brother had had this happen to him a few times before, and he simply decided, enough is enough. He was going to keep the pen and move on. The man followed us, getting very agitated, but my brother ignored him. As soon as this man raised his voice, something happened inside of me. I was terrified. I began to cry and beg my brother to give the pen back to him. Seeing my distress, he did so.

I couldn't explain to him why I had reacted in such an intense way. I only knew that when I was around anger or angry people, I feared for my survival.

FIRST FEARS

I had always had some understanding of why I was afraid of anger. But with the doctor and later with my mother I was able to walk beyond a painful, devastating period of my childhood—the year of my father's illness. One of the things that was most healing to me was my mom's presence in the hospital. In my first two weeks of inpatient treatment, I worked with the doctor alone. But later, in the second phase of my treatment, called Partial Hospitalization Program (PHP), my mother came to be with me.

Without my even asking, she flew over from Scotland and stayed for a month. I will be eternally grateful that I have a mother who has always made it easier for me to believe that God's love will never fail me, because her love never has. I know it was painful for her to sit in sessions with me and relive what were the hardest days of her life, but she did it unquestioningly because she knew it helped me.

When I look at pictures of me as a little girl before my father's illness, my eyes are full of mischief. As a preschool child, I was a tomboy, fearless and full of life. My mother declares that she didn't get to sit down till I was five years old. As a child I adored my father. He understood my tomboy ways and gave me space to fly. At this stage of my life, anything seemed possible. After my father's death, I was not so sure.

After my father suffered his brain thrombosis, his personality changed overnight. He went from being a warm, fun, kind dad to an angry, unpredictable stranger. It was as if his emotions were reversed—those he loved the most when he was himself, he seemed to *hate* the most when brain storms shook him. As a child, I actually feared for my life.

My father's death was devastating to me. I was too young to understand what had happened to him. All I knew was that at the end he seemed to be very angry with me, and then he was gone.

As adults we understand how the brain can be ravaged, changing a personality, but a child has no capacity for that kind of thinking. With the information I had as a four-year-old, I came to wrong conclusions about my life: I must have done something to make my father so angry. I was determined that no one would ever again be angry with me. I became a very good girl who never rocked the boat.

When I gave my life to Christ as an eleven-year-old, I was overwhelmed by the love and acceptance I felt from him. It became my life's work to never lose that love. But I always wondered, if those closest to you can change their minds, would it be possible to do something to lose the love of Jesus too? I had no idea what I had done to change my dad, so how would I know what would make God look away? As I grew and matured as a believer, I came to know that it was his grace alone that sustained me, but I never dealt with the roots of my passionate commitment to perfection, and they cast long shadows. I was afraid to be less than "the best."

As I grew up, I made a lot of good choices for bad reasons. I am glad that I did not rebel and walk away from God; I am happy that I threw myself into serving him. But I *am* sorry it took me so long to truly understand that "perfect love drives out fear" (1 John 4:18).

For me, the stakes got much higher as I became more recognizable. I enjoyed being president of the Junior Christian Endeavor at church, and it was fun to sing the lead role in the school musical, but as the years went on I invested more and more of myself into how I was received and perceived by the public. That became the plumb line to me; it measured the value of my life. I never wanted to rock the boat, so I never did.

As my life moved on and new opportunities were given me, my successes convinced me that I was okay. As I began to travel and speak and sing, it was amazing to me to watch people respond to the Lord working through me. When I would feel lost and alone, as if I did not belong anywhere, I was comforted by those who seemed to be helped. It gave me a sense of purpose, of definition, to know God was with me.

When it became apparent to me that my public minstry was coming to an end, and I could no longer keep going, my life felt empty and hopeless. When it became obvious I was letting people down and that some people seemed happy to see me falter, I felt terror.

TURNING POINT

"So, what is the worst thing that could happen to you, Sheila?" the doctor asked.

"I am afraid I will be swept away. I know there are a couple of people who would gladly destroy my life."

"Sheila, who is your trust in?" he asked me. "Do you feel as if the Lord has left you?" That question was a turning point in my journey, because my answer was a resounding no! I had written a poem in my journal the previous evening:

> *I never knew you lived so close to the floor,*
> *but every time I am bowed down,*
> *crushed by this weight of grief,*
> *I feel your hand on my head,*
> *your breath on my cheek,*
> *your tears on my neck.*
> *You never tell me to pull myself together,*
> *to stem the flow of many years.*
> *You simply stay by my side*
> *for as long as it takes,*
> *so close to the floor.*

Until this crisis I had never known what an awesome companion the Lord longs to be. I had spent so many years trying to make him proud of me, determined to never fail, that I missed the most amazing gift of all: to be able, as the British poet Stuart Henderson so eloquently wrote, "to bury my face in the mane of the Lion of Judah."

I watched *The Lion, the Witch and the Wardrobe* by C. S. Lewis again recently. There is so much to hear in children's stories. The part that is most memorable to me happens when the children are preparing to meet Aslan the lion for the very first time. They are afraid to come face-to-face with such powerful animal, and their guides acknowledge the appropriateness of that reaction. Susan says,

> "Is he—quite safe? I shall feel rather nervous about meeting a lion."

"That you will, dearie, and no mistake," said Mrs. Beaver. . . .

"Then he isn't safe?" said Lucy.

"Safe?" said Mrs. Beaver. " . . . 'Course he isn't safe. But he's good. He's the King."

Running to hide our faces in God is not like seeking the comfort and familiarity of a childhood blanket that allows us to tune out the realities of our lives. God is a mighty lion, whose roar is heard in every corner of the world. Still, when you are in trouble, you can hide your face from him or run to him and let him hide you in his mane. There you will find strength to live your life.

AGE-OLD FEARS

In the Bible fear is first mentioned in Genesis 3:10, when Adam said to the Lord, "I heard you in the garden, and I was afraid." Fear entered our world at the Fall. Adam was afraid because he knew he had disobeyed God. The peace and tranquillity of the Garden of Eden was lost forever. Once humankind had listened to the serpent, good and evil became players on our stage. From that point in human history, fear either threw us on our faces before God or caused us to hide our faces from him.

David was very familiar with fear. In Psalm 56:3 he wrote, "When I am afraid, I will trust in you," and he cried out in Psalm 69:1, "Save me, O God, for the waters have come up to my neck." He also wrote these magnificent, life-sustaining words:

The LORD is my light and my salvation—
whom shall I fear?
The LORD is the stronghold of my life—
of whom shall I be afraid?

PSALM 27:1

To David, fear was a reaction to forces that were coming against him; it was not a response, not a way of life. As an older man, he was able to deal with fear and the threats of his enemies because of how he lived as a young man. David had been a shepherd boy, whose job was to make sure no harm came to the sheep. From time to time lions or bears would try to carry a lamb away, but David was right there, slingshot in hand, ready to fight for the lamb's life. In the quiet, early years of his life, hidden away in a field, he made the choices to become the man he would later be. If David had run away as a boy, he would have run away as an adult; instead, he grabbed hold of his fear and reined it in.

FACING MY FEARS

Now it was my turn to rein in my fear. Courage is developed by embracing our greatest fears and not being deterred by them. I used to wait for courage, as if it were a gift that would be dropped by heaven into my heart, instantly transforming me into the kind of woman I imagined I could be.

But I had to start with the kind of woman that I was and, by pressing on, find courage. My favorite character in *The Wizard of Oz* is the Cowardly Lion. Underneath the false bravado, the Cowardly Lion is a very scared creature who believes that if he can just make it to the Emerald City, he will be home free. His expressed intention for the journey is to ask the wizard for the gift of courage. As he sets off on the journey with Dorothy, the Tin Man, the Scarecrow and Toto, he encounters all sorts of hazards. But because the travelers are committed to one another, they risk going beyond their comfort level. The Cowardly Lion does not allow his fear to disable him. By the time they discover that the wizard is just a man, he is no longer afraid.

In his book *Better Than Gold*, Edward Weeks quotes Eleanor Roosevelt who said,

> You gain strength, courage and confidence by
> every experience in which you really stop to look fear
> in the face. You are able to say to yourself, "I lived

through this horror; I can take the next thing that comes along. . . ." You must do the thing you think you cannot do.

That is how things began to change for me. I knew that in seeking my security and strength in the approval of others, I would rise or fall at their dictate. Fear of anger was making it easy for me to be controlled by angry people, but I must be controlled only by Christ.

I decided to start listening to what God had to say about my life. It was not easy, but I knew that it would give me courage to be real with other people, to be vulnerable. The Lord's love is a strong love that does not flatter or overlook our sinful nature: "For he knows how we are formed, he remembers that we are dust" (Psalm 103:14).

In the hospital, I began to pray the psalms out loud. David was passionately honest in his relationship with God. He did not close down as I had learned to do. I discovered what liberty lies in *voicing my fears*. I wrote:

Why do I shutter my heart?
Why do I keep it closed
on days when it seems about to break?
Why can't I let it go?
Why can't I ask for help
and admit that I'm barely alive?
I think if I voice it
I'd have to believe it
to hear all the sadness.
I just could not bear it.
That's why I shutter my heart.

While I used to be afraid to name my fear, as if voicing fears would make them more real and give them more power, I now discovered the opposite was true. I could scream aloud to the Lord and still be standing. I wasn't evaporated by my own words.

75

> *Fear of man will prove to be a snare,*
> *but whoever trusts in the LORD is kept safe.*
>
> PROVERBS 29:25

Fear still creeps up on me at times. I was at a movie a few weeks ago with my best friend. It was a thriller. The little theater was bursting with tension, popcorn uneaten. The murderer advanced upon his victim. Suddenly my friend leaned over and whispered menacingly in my ear. It was supposed to be funny—one of those moments when you jump and everyone laughs and the tension is relieved—but for that moment, I was overwhelmed with terror. I wanted to get up and run and hide. I was reduced in an instant to a terrified little girl. When incidents like this occur, I find that talking about my feelings to the Lord and to those who love me takes away fear's power to rule over me. I cry sometimes if that helps, but I remind myself whose I am. Fear still affects me—as it did King David—but it does not control me.

> *I sought the LORD, and he answered me;*
> *he delivered me from all my fears.*
>
> PSALM 34:4

FEAR OF INTIMACY

As I grew older, my childhood fear had grown into a general uneasiness and a mistrust of people. Fear and intimacy do not make good traveling companions, so I lived a very busy, crowded, solitary life.

I had felt so alone for so long. Now I began to understand that the greatest barrier to intimacy is fear—fear of being known, fear of being rejected, fear of facing the truth about ourselves. John Donne, the sixteenth-century poet, wrote these familiar but profound words:

> No man is an island, entire of itself; every man is
> a piece of the continent, a part of the main. . . . Any
> man's death diminishes me because I am involved in

mankind, and therefore never send to know for whom
the bell tolls; it tolls for thee.

What Donne showed in that masterly quote is a deep
spiritual truth: We are involved in one another's lives. Yet he
hints at a human problem: At times a fear of connection
drives us away from one another. We are afraid to be known
because we might be rejected. We are afraid to be known
because at some deep level we fear that the truth about us,
when out in the open and reflected back to us through someone else's eyes, will be shocking to *ourselves*. So we struggle with this human dichotomy; we long to be known
because we are lonely, and we fear being known because we
may then be loneliest of all.

FEAR OF DISAPPROVAL OR FAILURE

Part of coming to terms with fear has been accepting
that there is good and bad in me and good and bad in others.
Jesus' statement "Pray for your enemies" presupposes that
enemies exist. We do have enemies, people who would
rather see us fail than succeed. We know too, from the story
of Job, that at times God will allow our lives to be disrupted.
The lesson for me is that God is passionately committed to
the kind of woman that I *become*, not to what I *do*.

This simple truth has revolutionized my life. It is the
opposite of what we hear on television or read about in the
newspaper, and is contrary to what we in the church seem
to believe as well. We place so much emphasis on success
and achievement, on accomplishment and numbers. But
God is singularly unimpressed with all the paraphernalia we
have attached to our faith.

I am learning that what God cares about is who I am
when the lights are off and the crowds have gone home. It
also means that whatever comes into my life, whether it is
what I would choose or not, can be used by the Lord to mold
my life if I will rest in him.

I used to live in fear, wondering what might happen to me, what someone might say about me. But now, as Thomas à Kempis said in *The Imitation of Christ*, I am learning to "receive all things from the hand of God. From his justice and from his bounty with humble submission to his blessed will."

One of the greatest gifts God would give us is peace of mind. Perhaps, like me, you feel you need to find a desert island if you want to remain at peace. The demands of our lives constantly pester us, like flies on a hot summer day. But even though life is difficult and demanding, it remains true that the perfect love of Jesus has the power to drive out our most devastating fears.

While at the hospital, I still had many questions about my future. I did not know where I would go when I left there—if I would return to CBN or leave Virginia Beach. As I looked to the future, I felt like a tiny boat on rough seas, but at least I was beginning to understand I was not alone in the boat.

FEAR AND ANGER

As I looked at how my fear had manifested itself over the years, I realized that, even though I was afraid of anger in others, I responded to that fear with, yes, anger. Silent anger. I used it as protection, a shield to hide behind.

One writer has compared repressed anger to having a basement full of pent-up, angry dogs. I like that illustration, for that is just how it felt to me. What made it worse was that I must have somehow snuck in the dogs when no one was looking. After all, I am a Christian woman, and women are not supposed to be angry.

If a man is angry he is often viewed as a man of passion, of principle, but an angry woman is quite another matter. It is too easy to dismiss her as neurotic or strident, and if she happens to be single, well, she may as well be quiet and break out the knitting!

Anger born out of pain needs to find a place of release, but how do women do that? Many of us struggle with anger that has little to do with righteousness. I don't think that I have ever heard a sermon on how to handle anger, even though I believe we have churches full of angry people.

As I sat in a group meeting at the hospital one morning, talking about some of the most painful experiences of my life, someone said, "You sound very detached, Sheila. Some of this stuff is pretty recent. Why aren't you angry?"

I was shocked and disturbed by what this other patient was saying.

He continued, "You sound like you are telling someone else's story. Don't you care about your life?"

I did not say much more that morning, but for the rest of the day, it was as if I were running old black-and-white movies of my life through my head.

My first taste of anger—from my father to me as a child—had affected my whole life. I would do anything I could to diffuse an angry situation. Angry words or tone of voice—spoken even by myself—seemed to me to signal something drastic about to happen. I never gave myself permission to be angry; when things happened in my life that I should have been angry about, I just stuffed the feelings down. I packed the cellar as tightly as I could, ground my teeth and clenched my fists and said nothing. Occasionally, when I wasn't being vigilant, little bits would escape, leaking out in sudden outbursts or sarcasm, but I seldom threw those dogs any meat at all. The hungrier they got, the more they fought to escape, the more I guarded them. I talked louder or worked harder until they tired of their barking and quieted down for a while.

FACING MY ANGER

It is very difficult to begin to deal with these issues when you are thirty-five and not fifteen. In the hospital I wrote down everything I could think of that I was angry about. But I didn't know what to do with it. So I began to pray. I felt as if the Lord was the only one who could deal with the waves of emotion that were sweeping over me and not be diminished by them.

Once again, the Psalms modeled raw emotion for me. One from the days of Israel's captivity in Babylon contains some of the strongest language in the Bible:

> *Oh Daughter of Babylon, doomed to*
> *destruction,*
> *happy is he who repays you*
> *for what you have done to us—*
> *he who seizes your infants*
> *and dashes them against the rocks.*
>
> PSALM 137:8–9

Strong words from God's people. Several editions of prayer books or worship books have edited these words out. Eugene Peterson, in his book *Answering God*, says that these "Psalmectomies" are wrong, reasoning: "They are wrong-headed because our hate needs to be prayed, not suppressed."

What a liberating concept: that our hate—our anger—needs to be prayed. Burying it will not make it go away. Suppressing it contaminates our souls. If we fail to take it to God, it will leak out and destroy the world.

As I began to look at my own life, to listen to the things that made me angry, I realized that *my anger always sprang out of fear.* When I felt I was being threatened in some way, I became angry in order to defend myself—the dogs of rage would rise up to my defense. It was as if my trust was in the sheepdog, not the Shepherd. The sheepdog looked ready to devour anything that invaded his land, so I stuck close to him. Anger offered me a way of gaining control when I felt out of control.

I am learning now to trust the Shepherd to be my defender. For me it is a daily, sometimes hourly, relinquishing of control of my life and my destiny to God. When I feel myself getting angry now, I take a step back. I go into another room by myself, sit at the Shepherd's feet, and I tell him what I am feeling. When I forget to do that, or choose not to do that, I ask for forgiveness. I do not take this lightly. It is no fun to be the recipient of my anger. Scripture, in fact, tells us to avoid such people (Proverbs 22:24).

For any number of reasons, many of us live on the edge of a volcano. So I say with Eugene Peterson, let's pray our anger out; let's cry our hurt and pain and fear until we have no tears left. Anger needs to be expressed, and it is much better for us to cry it out to God than to machine-gun our friends with it.

One of the most wonderful aspects of our relationship with Christ is that we don't have to talk—he understands. When you are in pain it is so exhausting to have to try and explain to others what you are feeling. What a relief it is to be able to lay down in a field with the Shepherd and not have to say a word.

There is a mystery at play here: the broken bread principle. Remember the story? A little boy brings his lunch to Jesus, who blesses it, breaks it, and passes it out to his friends to distribute to the crowd. A miracle occurs. One boy's lunch multiplies and feeds four thousand people. There is enough for everyone.

We can allow fear and anger to cripple our souls, or we can bring our devastating circumstances to Christ and ask him to bless us in our brokenness and to feed his body, the church. Shortly after hymn writer George Matheson became engaged to be married, he lost his eyesight. His fiancée left him. Facing loss and an unknown future, he could have become a bitter, angry man. I would imagine that he tasted both bitterness and anger, but he did not feast on them or let them feast on him. He took his burden to Christ, and you and I are fed by his words:

O Love that will not let me go
I rest my weary soul in thee
I give thee back the life I owe
that in thine ocean depths its flow
may richer, fuller be.
O Joy that seekest me through pain
I cannot close my heart to thee
I trace the rainbow through the rain
and feel the promise is not vain
that morn shall tearless be.

We are people who need each other. We need each other to be honest, to struggle with the pain of life, to look for traces of redemption in the darkest moments. And if the whole purpose of our lives on this earth is to glorify God and enjoy him forever, then I believe he is the one to whom we can bring the emotions that tear at our hearts. As we bare our souls before him, he will trade our unbearable burdens for a load that we can carry.

Father God, hear our prayers.
We bring our fear to you.
We bring our rage to you.
We bring the broken pieces of our lives.
Teach us to live lightly,
casting our cares on you.
Thank you that we can bury our faces in you.
Amen.

Fear and shame have clothed me
like a suit of cheap perfume—
impossible to point to,
but felt in every room.

6

Paralyzed by Shame

I lugged around inside me a dead weight
of not-good-enoughness.
LEWIS SMEDES,
SHAME AND GRACE

It was always spring in the garden. Every morning the
sweet perfume of a hundred different flowers melted
together to create the fragrance of the day. The sun was
warm and gentle. Each new day was filled with endless possibilities; good things rested under every leaf. Animals
leaned on one another as they napped at peace in the shade
of a tree. This was a paradise.

A golden cord ran through the hearts of Adam and Eve
that also touched the trees, the flowers, the animals. Nothing was untouched by the cord that led back to the Lord of
the garden. Adam and Eve were asleep when the serpent
approached them. He began to sing a different song, a
strange song, discordant with the melody of the garden. It
woke them up. "There is more," he whispered to them, "so
much more."

Eve looked at the strange creature. It was hard to see
him clearly because the sun was in her eyes.

"There is more. There is much more. He is keeping
things from you. You are not all you could be."

What could he possibly mean, more?

"You know so little, child," the serpent said pityingly. "It's there for the taking."

Eve looked at the serpent; she looked at the tree. God had told them to stay away. Now she wondered why. If this truly was their garden, surely they could do what they wanted. Eve stretched her hand toward the fruit. Not an animal moved. She took it and bit into it—a sweet, strong taste.

She gave some to Adam. "Taste this. This is better than all the rest."

Adam raised the fruit to his lips and let the juice run down his face. Just then the sun vanished behind a cloud and the animals ran for cover. Some of the smaller creatures were crushed in the scuffle, but no one even noticed. Eve felt a chill in the air. She and Adam looked at each other, and they knew that something was wrong, very wrong. So little had happened, but everything was different. The moment they decided to taste the part of life they were missing, everything changed. Their eyes were "opened," and what they saw horrified them.

They turned away from one another and quickly assembled garments made of fig leaves to cover themselves. But it wasn't enough; they still felt naked. All day they hid under the cover of a tree, but in the evening, they heard God's voice. He was asking for them, asking why they were hiding.

Adam and Eve tried to hide under layers of clothing. We have been adding to those layers ever since, not in clothing but in layer upon layer of internal veiling. Even Adam and Eve felt the new, unfamiliar feeling that sat, heavy as a stone, inside both of them. They did not know its name, but we do: It is called shame.

Until that cataclysmic moment, they had trusted one another. Then, suddenly, sin caused them to hide from God and from each other. I believe that the seeds of all of our relational ills can be seen in this Genesis story. Sin brought us into a world of fear, a fear closely linked to shame.

I have read several books on shame, which seems to be defined in a variety of ways. Most people distinguish between guilt and shame, defining guilt as the feeling that accompanies having *done* something wrong, and shame as the feeling that you *are* something wrong.

SHAME'S DEEP ROOTS

Where would I start to explain to you a feeling that is as familiar to me as my face in the mirror? For as long as I can remember, I have felt the breath of the racehorse Shame on my neck. We are old traveling companions. I can be as impatient as anyone else with the "I tripped over my dog when I was two, and I will never be able to trust again" rhetoric of pop psychology. I do know, however, that the significant events of early life have the power to shape our futures.

Look through my window for a moment, and you will see a very happy family: a loving mother and father, three children, and a little brown dachshund. Suddenly, overnight, everything is changed. A blood clot wipes out a part of the father's brain and the picture of "normal" is gone.

For a while after the immediate crisis, my father was able to be at home with us. Dark storms blew through his mind—and our house. What I saw in his eyes in those darker moments, I will carry with me for years. I truly believed that at a core level I was a bad person. How else could I explain why someone who loved me suddenly turned on me in rage?

It became apparent that having my father at home was not a safe choice for anyone. He was soon gone, and within a year he had died while in a hospital. The puppy was gone too, because it needed too much care during this time of crisis.

Life moved from safe to scary overnight. I—the younger daughter—fell from being invincible to having to protect myself at all costs. *Don't let anyone see inside*, I would tell myself. *Perhaps someone will see whatever it*

*was that your daddy saw. Perhaps that person will leave—
and you know how much that hurts.*

Although I know now that there was nothing for my
dad to see, I did not know that then.

In the hospital, with my mom at my side, I relived these
childhood events. So often we perceive pain as a negative
force to be avoided at all costs. But just as the pain of child-
birth brings new life into the world, so the pain of walking
through the darkest valleys brings the traveler to the land that
lies beyond. As Mom and I talked through the times I had tried
to erase from my mind, I was able to bring adult perspective
to childhood pain. Just to hear from someone that I love and
trust that what had happened with my dad was not my fault,
that he loved me very much and would have been proud of
me, was like bathing tired feet in warm oil.

NOT UP TO STANDARD

As I allowed this fresh perspective to take center stage
for a while, I saw how for so long I had been chasing the
image of a perfect china cup. Let me explain. When I was a
student in London, I bought a china cup from the Reject
China Shop. It was only a few doors away from Harrod's
magnificent department store, and it stocked the items that
did not quite meet Harrod's standard. Sometimes if you
looked hard enough, you could find a piece that seemed perfect. I was sure I had found such a piece; it must have
slipped through quality control. I held it up to the light and
couldn't see a single flaw.

With some pride in my find, I took it home and put on
the kettle to make some tea and christen my cup. But as
soon as I poured the boiling liquid into the cup, the china
cracked from top to bottom. The flaw that was impercepti-
ble to the human eye was exposed by the heat of the water.

That was how I felt about my life. On the outside,
everything looked great. But if it ever got too hot, I was sure

I would crack from top to bottom. I had felt this way for as long as I could remember.

My first taste of "fame" was at a Christian holiday camp in England. I was twenty-four years old and employed by British Youth For Christ as a musical evangelist. My normal role was to support other musicians and help lead worship, but for this camp I was asked to prepare a solo concert with the band. Graham Kendrick and a few other friends wrote songs for me. I thought it was going to be fun until the night approached. I suddenly realized that if the concert was a disaster, I stood alone.

I was petrified. The day came, and the auditorium was packed. I had recorded two of my songs on a "single," and the record company was there that night for the debut. Before I went on, I sat backstage with my head between my knees. I felt as if I would either vomit or pass out, but there was no time for either. I heard them announce my name.

The concert went incredibly well. I left the stage relieved and thinking that now I would go out with my friends for a burger just as we always had before. But no. I was whisked off to the record table to sign records. They sold out that evening, and everyone was exuberant. I had wanted my life to be used by God, and this seemed to be the breakthrough we had been looking for.

I had never experienced that kind of manic attention before. Everything changed for me that night. Christian magazines wanted to do interviews. Radio stations wanted my opinion on everything. I was no longer just a person; I was "special." At least, that is how it seemed to me. I soon received invitations to sing all over the country.

Even though that first concert went very well, it did not help my anxiety the next time or the time after that. I was very nervous, so I began to concentrate on the exterior of my life. If I had to meet with a record company representative or an interviewer, I bought a new outfit. I did not make a lot of money with YFC, so I opened store credit cards. I couldn't bear to face new people unless I had carefully wrapped up the outside of my life.

As time moved on, the stakes got much higher. And some internal sense of radar also got much more sensitive. The more unsure I felt about myself, the more I picked up on people's reactions to me. I took things personally that I should have been able to slough off.

A few years later, I was invited to meet with a producer from the BBC television network in London. They were looking for a host for a new show, representing the best of contemporary Christian and traditional black gospel music. I was chosen as the new host.

Before the first show, makeup artists and wardrobe people fussed over me endlessly. We taped the show, and it aired a few nights later. I remember sitting with a bunch of friends watching it. It looked all right to me, until one of my friends' six-year-old son said, "Wow, you look a lot fatter on television!"

Everyone laughed, and I did too, but I was dying inside.

A few weeks later, I was on the studio floor with the band, rehearsing, and suddenly over the whole audio system I heard the director yell, "Makeup! Do something with her ears." The makeup girl ran out and fussed a bit with my hair and then yelled into my microphone, "I'm a makeup artist, not a miracle worker!"

For the rest of the day, every time I turned around, someone was looking at my ears. I could have sold tickets. Afterwards, I asked the girl what was wrong with my ears.

"They stick out, dear."

Someone else added, "We better make sure that there are no strong winds in the studio!"

Everyone went off laughing, and I went to my dressing room and wept.

The next day I looked in the yellow pages for plastic surgeons. I found one clinic close to where I was living. I called and asked how much it would be to have my ears pinned back. She gave me two prices, one for a general anesthetic and one for a local. Because I already felt guilty about spending money on something like that, I went for the local. I was petrified. I hate the sight of blood, particularly mine, but my mind was set. As they wheeled me into the operating room, I prayed that God would not let them mess up and cut my ears off!

The surgery was horrible. They gave me four injections in each ear and then began to cut. I passed out on the spot, so the general anesthetic would have been a waste of money! I left the hospital with a numb face and my head wrapped in bandages, but convinced that I would now feel better about myself.

I did not. My ears were no longer the focal point of the show, but when deep distress is internal, you cannot heal that with surgery.

I remember one more encounter: I was standing at a cosmetic counter in Harrod's, waiting to pay for a tube of lipstick, when a girl asked for my autograph. People turned to look and see who I was. I smiled, signed my name, and gave the girl the piece of paper. She looked at it and said, "What does that bit at the bottom say?"

"Sheila Walsh," I answered.

"Oh, man, I thought you were Sheena Easton," she said in disgust as she threw the paper away. My self-esteem went down yet another peg.

Deep down I believed that my imperfections had made my father turn from me. If I could just seem flawless to myself, to God, and to others—like a perfect Harrod's china cup—I would be loved. The truth I was beginning to realize in the hospital is that Christ is the only perfect cup.

THE SHAME PROFILE

While in the hospital, I had the opportunity to attend a talk on the subject of shame. As the psychologist outlined the "shame profile," many of us shifted uncomfortably in our chairs. This is what it looks like:

1. *Shame includes an enduring negative self-image.* No matter how many wonderful things are happening in your life, none of it means anything to you because of how you feel about yourself, inside.

2. *Shame is highly "performance conscious."* You always feel you are "on." You are so anxious to please and to be needed that you measure your worth by what you can produce, as if that will give you value in the eyes of yourself and others.

3. *Shame makes you unaware of personal boundaries.* You're not sure who you are as separate from someone else; you're not sure where you "end" and others "begin." You find it virtually impossible to stand up for yourself and say no. It's easier to allow others to make decisions and choose for you. You reveal inappropriate personal details of your life to people whom you have only recently met, in an attempt to feel connected to someone.

4. *Shame festers in people who are "wounded."* Underneath the surface of your life, there is a wound that has never healed. You nurse it and maintain it. It gives you identity.

5. *Shame is accompanied by a pervading tiredness.* There is no place for joy in shame. This means you are always tired and weighed down by life. Burdens overwhelm you.

6. *Shame has a built-in radar system, tuned to keeping everyone happy and at peace.* A sense of shame makes you overly responsible. You make it your job to ensure everything is running smoothly and everyone else is happy.

7. *Shame makes you ignore your own needs like a martyr.* Because shame tells you that you are no good, you seek to balance the scales by ignoring your own legiti-

mate needs. Attempts to please and appease others are always more important than listening to and caring for yourself.

8. *Shame tends toward addictive behavior, which can manifest itself in overinvolvement in work or ministry.* You are so ashamed of yourself that you work harder and longer in a desperate search for that elusive peace. (This is a huge issue in the church.)

9. *Shame has no concept of "normal."* If you have grown up with unhealthy behavior in your family, you perceive that to be the norm. You lack the perspective to know what "normal" should look like. For example, if you grew up with someone yelling in your face, that became familiar to you; you don't realize it is unhealthy behavior you do not have to live with.

10. *Shame makes it difficult to trust others.* You tend to be very guarded around others, wondering what their agenda is for your life. It is hard to let anyone in, because you're sure that person will not like what she sees. This behavior can border on paranoia.

11. *Shame makes you possessive in relationships.* Out of a feeling of unworthiness and fear of abandonment, you cling to the people in your life, afraid that if they leave, no one will be there to take their place.

12. *Shame has a high need for control.* Life is scary to a shame-based person; the only bearable way to survive is to maintain control.

It is easy to see why wounded people adopt some of these patterns. If the one who should protect you from pain (such as a parent or spouse) becomes the perpetrator of the pain, it is easiest to throw up walls, so you won't be hurt again in the future; trust becomes a major issue.

I recognized myself in many of the points discussed that evening. I had never heard of personal boundaries (we don't have those in Scotland!), but as I listened to what was being said, it began to make sense to me. For example, I have had a very difficult time developing intimate relationships with a few close friends. I kept my true self pretty guarded and safe. But if you talked to viewers of "The 700 Club," they would probably disagree, saying that I am a very open person whom they know well. The strange thing is, it felt safe to unburden my soul to a large, anonymous crowd, much safer than to a few people who really knew me. I now think I sometimes shared things with our viewers that were really not television fare.

SHAME, GUILT, AND SHAMELESSNESS

Shame is so dehumanizing. There is no dignity or strength in shame. It tells us that we are worthless and hopeless. Shame is much more damaging than good old-fashioned guilt because it seems so hopeless. If we have *done* something wrong, we can make an active attempt to rectify the situation. But if we *are* something wrong, what hope is there?

As I uncovered the shame that had drawn me in like quicksand, I also realized that, though it was important that I understand my past, I could not *blame* my past. Shifting the blame will never make anything better. It is only as I step up to the plate and accept full responsibility for my life that I will ever find peace and healing.

Again, I note that there is a great difference between the unhealthy shame that makes us crawl away into a corner and the kind of healthy shame—called guilt—that shows us when we are wrong and need to change our ways. The Bible calls us to live with integrity and humility, constantly confessing our sins to one another and loving one another. But it's important to remember that this biblical call to face our sins and our human frailties is neither the shame that makes us feel as if we must run and hide our brokenness, nor a shamelessness that tries to release us from any accountability to anyone or anything.

The February 6, 1995, issue of *Newsweek* featured an interesting cover story titled "The Return of Shame." One only has to watch our talk shows for a few moments to see how shameless we have become. After working in my office late one evening, I picked up the remote control and flicked through the channels to see if I could find something fun on television to unwind with before I went to bed. I was looking for "The Lucy Show," but that was not what I found. The talk show had already started when I tuned in, but it soon became apparent that the subject was "Married couples who are looking to make it a threesome." The thing that made me so sad was that the couple onstage when I tuned in were a thirty-eight-year-old woman and her eighty-three-year-old husband. I looked at this man who could have been my grandfather, and I wanted to grab hold of him and shake him and ask him where his dignity had gone. In its article *Newsweek* called for "a means of provoking shame rooted in hardheaded compassion, the results of which would be redemptive."

This is an acutely felt need. I saw a story on CNN recently that was capturing the aftermath of a murder trial in Philadelphia. The reporter was interviewing the mother of the young victim. She had such a ravaged look on her face. The reporter asked her if she was glad that it was all over and that a conviction had been brought in. She didn't say anything for a moment; then she said, "Do you know what that boy said to me? He said, 'So what if I killed your son?' My baby is gone, and that is all he had to say."

Tears rolled down my cheeks as I saw the look of utter disbelief in the eyes of this bereaved mother, numbed by the indifference of a cold-blooded killer.

I stand with *Newsweek* in a call to accountability, but I see very little hope for the tide to be turned; the only hope is the church, but I wonder if we, as the church, are looking in the right direction.

IT IS NOT OUR JOB TO SHAME THE WORLD

Jesus never shamed anyone. He called some of the church leaders on their hypocrisy. He was angry when they turned a sanctuary into a marketplace. But he never shamed people.

Remember the scene where a crowd of religious men threw a woman at Jesus' feet, demanding their pound of flesh. She had been caught in adultery and by law should have been stoned to death. Jesus said to them, "All right, if that is how you want to handle this, then let's spray everyone with the same dye. If you have never sinned, please feel free to throw the first stone." Slowly the crowd slipped away and left the woman lying in the dust. Jesus picked her up and said to her, "They have all gone home. No one is left to accuse you, and neither do I—but don't do this anymore; you are worth more than this." (I have paraphrased this story from John 8.) Jesus also treated Mary Magdalene with respect and dignity. And even when he was being tortured to death, Jesus had time for the thief dying beside him.

Christ recognized what we have forgotten: that every single human being on this planet has been created in the *imago dei*, the image of God. Talk show hosts and their nutty guests, women who stream into abortion clinics, gay rights activists who yell in our faces, *must* be treated with dignity and respect, because the mark of the image of God rests upon us all, no matter how defaced it might be.

I sense that the church devotes too much time trying to keep the mud of the world off "our" shoes and too little time washing it off "theirs." As long as we simply point fingers, why should anyone listen to us? It is not our job to try and shame the world, but to love them with the love of Christ. After Jesus looked at a man or a woman, he or she was never the same again. It makes me sad that it seems Christians' voices are heard publicly only when we are against something. Yes, we are living in a very sick and depraved world. But will we draw people to us and to Christ if we stand and tell the world they have brought their pain upon themselves and walk away without helping them?

Christ spoke the truth in all its heartbreaking power to everyone he encountered. Jesus even left the crowd to have dinner with a tax collector who had been ripping people off for years. We don't know what was said, but we do know that, after this encounter with Jesus, the tax collector was a changed man. His heart was so transformed that he not only repaid what he had stolen from others, he paid back four times what he had taken and then gave half of his wealth to the poor (Luke 19:1–10). Jesus took the fierce and piercing light of who he is to every situation, but he went in love.

WHEN A CHRISTIAN FALTERS

We come to Christ to be forgiven for our sins, to be given a new heart, and then we are asked to care for one another, to be the church. But too often the church doesn't know how to be the church. In his book *Guilt and Grace*, Paul Tournier wrote:

> The church proclaims the grace of God and moralism, which is the negation of it, always creeps back into its bosom. Grace becomes conditional. Judgment appears. I see its ravages every day in all the Christian churches.

By our behavior, Christians say to one another that as long as we are all performing "normally," we will walk together. But if one of us stumbles, then the rest of us will simply keep walking, praying that we will learn to be better judges of character next time. We allow our disappointment to become distance, confirming the worst fears of the person who is left lying in the dust: "I am a bad person; why did I even hope that God could love me?"

The words of St. Paul have been very helpful to me. Even though he was being used in unprecedented ways to build up the fledgling church, Paul still struggled with his sinful nature. "For what I do is not the good I want to do; no, the evil I do not want to do—this I keep on doing" (Romans 7:19). Paul made it very clear that we are in a battle with our nature and that, at times, that sinful nature will win out. Paul never used that as an excuse, however; he continued to press on to be more like Christ.

I cry for mercy for those in the dust, and yet I understand the fears of those who wonder what we, as Christians, are supposed to do about the sin and confusion among us.

Too often we Christians see only two possibilities for dealing with human frailty: (1) we distance ourselves from those who are in trouble, in the earnest desire that this will wake them up and they will straighten themselves out; (2) we ignore the warnings we note in others' lives in a desire to respect their privacy. I suggest a third way: that we speak the truth to one another, that we care enough to reach out, and that, no matter what we find, we do not let go.

Like a mother sending her daughter off to college for the first time, Paul is very careful to instruct the church in how to deal with problems that will inevitably occur. "Brothers, if someone is caught in a sin, you who are spiritual should restore him gently. But watch yourself, or you also may be tempted. Carry each other's burdens, and in this way you will fulfill the law of Christ" (Galatians 6:1–2).

It was interesting to me to note that the Greek word we translate as *restore* is the same word that would be used in a hospital setting if someone were brought in with a broken limb; it denotes brokenness and the need for time and care.

It is also interesting that Paul's words do not come across as a suggestion, but as a command. At times we are reluctant to get involved when someone is in trouble because we do not know what to say. While I can certainly relate to that, it is not scriptural. Other times we do not reach out because the person's trouble is too much like our own, and his or her struggle is rocking our boat. And sometimes we simply have no mercy, or it would demand too much of us to try and get involved.

As I write this book, I have watched some Christian public figures deal with crises lived out in a public spotlight. How have we, as the church, struggled to come to terms with what was revealed about these people? How should we deal with these crises? I have noticed a variety of responses to these people in crisis:

1. We must save their careers at all cost.
2. We should fix their problems quickly and quietly, behind the scenes.
3. Let's decide who is going to be the winner and who is going to be the loser, and back the winner.
4. The quick fixes are not working, so let's walk away.
5. We should say we saw it coming.
6. Let's move on with our lives and leave them in the dust.

I saw a television special on Mike Tyson the other evening. It made me think that we in the Christian community do not deal with each other very differently than the world deals with its heroes. It was very clear to those around Mike Tyson that he was a man filled with rage, but that very rage made him a killer boxer, so instead of caring for him, they marketed and sold his flaw.

I wonder if Christians are very different. We see what is happening behind the scenes with a person in public life, but that person is so effective at what he or she does, so powerful that we turn a blind eye. We reason away our concern by telling ourselves, "God is using that person." Well, God spoke through Balaam's ass, so I don't find that argument very convincing!

The problem that I have with the above situation is that it shows no love whatsoever toward the person in trouble. We walk with them for as long as we can until the situation blows up in our faces, and then we move on, leaving one more broken, used-up life in our wake.

Before I entered the hospital, many friends at CBN saw the pain in my face and simply stayed away. I know that divorce is a sin, and I understand that it was heartbreaking for those who knew me to see that become a reality in my life, but as much as I liked to avoid anger, I found it easier to deal with those who were at least openly angry and confused than with those who simply stopped calling. I read their distance as an assent to my belief that I was simply a bad person.

Many of these same people have since said they are sorry, that they just did not know what to say, and I have come to believe that the experience was good for all of us—after all, how else will we grow? Failure can be an awesome teacher if we invite Christ into the process. It was good for me that my friends distanced themselves, because it ultimately forced me to face my terrible fear of rejection and bring it to Jesus. It was good for them too, because it caused them to examine how we react to a life in crisis. (In falling short, we can ask the Lord to teach us how to be, so that the next time someone is in pain, we will be better equipped to deal with it.) But at the time, the silence I encountered added to my feelings of utter hopelessness. I had failed, therefore I was a failure. The hopelessness I felt was so pervasive that I ignored the calls of one old friend who wanted to come see me. I felt so ashamed that I could not look at anyone.

SHAME AND GRACE

Too many of us are at war within ourselves. When that is the case, the following questions arise: How can you extend grace to others when you have not received it yourself? Where do you go when you feel flawed? Where do you find healing when you know you are sick?

For me, the only place to go was to the feet of the only One who is perfect, the only One who fully understands how flawed I am and yet who loves me completely.

Jesus said, "Come to me, all you who are weary and burdened, and I will give you rest" (Matthew 11:28). When our Lord was being brutally executed, he was taking upon himself all the filth and decay of a diseased world. He knew that we could not make it on our own, so he took our place. Wherever he encountered darkness, he brought light. When he met people who were in hiding, he called them out. Whether it was a "scarlet woman" or a little man hiding up a tree, his words were words of healing and hope and freedom. Isaiah told us, "The people walking in darkness have seen a great light; on those living in the land of the shadow of death a light has dawned" (Isaiah 9:2).

I have a friend who is a missionary on the border between Thailand and Cambodia. One of his concerns is for people suffering from leprosy in the refugee camps. He and his colleagues began to spend time with those men and women, doing what they could to aid them physically and spiritually. Eventually a church was born, right there in the middle of a leper camp. During one of their services, a man who had been among the first to make a commitment to following Christ said, "One of the most wonderful things that has happened to me since I met Jesus is that now I can look you in the face. I was too ashamed before because of my disfigurement, but if Jesus loves me so much, then I think that I can hold my head up high."

That is how it is supposed to be for us all. Jesus has restored our dignity. What we sold so cheaply in Eden, he has bought back for us at a great price. We all struggle with our humanity, with our soulishness, but cleansing is not found in the shadows; it is found in the burning light.

Many people are afraid to get help because they fear it may cost them too much. And it may—it may cost you everything you have. That very fear ran through my mind time and again before I decided to get help. What if in reaching out for help myself, I discovered I was no longer welcome to reach out to others? My whole life had been focused on being a minister of Christ's love to a broken world.

Driving myself to the hospital, I knew those days might well be over. That seemed like a terrible thing to me, but I came to realize that when something is clearly revealed to you as the right thing to do and is supported by godly people that you respect, you run to it with all your strength and leave the rest to God. If God was finished using me in public ministry, then woe to me or anyone who tried to revive what he had stopped. But if God still had something for me to do, then all the armies of the world could not stop him.

Everyone's story is different. Perhaps you have been told you should never have been born, that you were a mistake. Perhaps you were told you would never amount to anything. So many things that happen to us as children leave greasy fingerprints on our souls. Children who have been beaten feel at some level that they deserve their beatings; those who have been sexually abused become accustomed to equating anything sexual with "love." Yet Jesus said he came to give us abundant life, life running over at the edges, more than we could ever imagine.

When you step out from the shadows into the storm, you may be at the mercy of the wind for a while, but Christ is Lord over the wind and the storms, and you will be truly alive—not just a whisper of who God called you to be. There is so much more to life than mere survival! God wants you to *live*, not just get through one more day. We can try in vain to fix ourselves, but only the One who made us knows the path to healing.

> *[I] will keep you and will make you to be a covenant for the people . . . , to open eyes that are blind, to free captives from prison and to release from the dungeon those who sit in darkness.*
>
> ISAIAH 42:6–7

When you find yourself at an emotional crossroads, you have to choose whether you will push your emotions down one more time, dismissing them as lightly as a summer cold, or will you stop and listen and ask God to help you understand why your life is so painful? Perhaps, like me, you will find things out about yourself that are disappointing. I, for instance, am learning to distinguish between healthy shame that alerts me to areas of my life that need to change and the unhealthy ocean of shame that does not belong to me. At times you may be overwhelmed with sadness, but if you are willing to sing its song for a little while, a great burden will be cut from you and roll down the mountain.

> *Lord Jesus,*
> *your love for me is beyond my understanding.*
> *I am so ashamed of what I bring to you today—*
> *my fears, my shame, my hopelessness.*
> *Today I choose to come out of the shadows*
> *into your light,*
> *into your healing,*
> *into your hope,*
> *into your life.*
> *Amen.*

FAREWELL LESSON

Let me end this chapter on shame with a scene that took place on my last day in the hospital. I had come a long way in revising my self-image, but I still had a long way to go.

I was sitting outside with my group enjoying an unexpected Indian summer day. Our staff group leader spoke up, "Sheila is leaving us today, and I want you all to give her some input as to what you perceive her strengths to be."

I could have died! I was very uncomfortable with the idea that everyone was expected to say something nice about me. I stared at my feet.

"You seem a little uncomfortable with this, Sheila," she said. "Why?"

"Well, you are forcing people to find something good about me. It seems a little staged."

She continued, "So, is there nothing good to say?"

"Well sure, but I have spent so much of my life trying to make people like me . . . I guess I'm not sure I really trust their perspective," I said.

"You have sat here every day with us and listened to input about your weaknesses. You've never resisted that. I think we would like to tell you what we see in you that we really like. Is that okay?" she asked.

"I guess so," I whispered.

"I see you as strong and compassionate," someone said.

"You make me laugh!" another added.

"I find it comforting to be around you," someone said. "You have a tender heart."

It was one of the most humbling experiences of my life, to look into the faces of people with whom I had gone through so much and listen to their positive appraisals. I had spent a month looking at my weaknesses. All I had wanted to do was to confess my failures to the Lord and then go and live quietly somewhere. I saw myself working in an art gallery or an antique shop in a small, sleepy town, where each Sunday I would go and take my place in church, grateful to God that he loved me and accepted me.

The group leader interrupted my thoughts. "You need to stop trying to control what is happening around you, Sheila. Be aware of other people, and don't let your pride stand in the way of someone being able to say, 'Thank you, you have made a difference in my life.'"

That is part of what it means to live beyond the shame profile. That is the new road I set out to travel. For years, I had denied that shame had a choke hold on my life, but till the day I die and beyond, I will thank God that he allowed me to finally see the shame for what it is and walk away from it.

It keeps me walking on the line;
it holds me to the flame,
yet makes me smile as if
my blistered flesh can feel no pain.
It pulls me far away
from those whose hands I long to hold;
it keeps me safe;

it keeps me winter cold.
So now I choose to walk away
from what I know so well.
I leave behind this Judas seed
and all the lies I tell,
and as I stand with empty hands
upon this valley floor,
I ask, dear Jesus,
walk me through this door.

Silence.
I hear my breath,
but nothing else.
The world is quiet.
I am alone.
Someone turned the lights out
and everyone went home.

7

The Longest Night

It is not for the moment that you are stuck
that you need courage, but for the long,
uphill climb back to sanity and security.
ANNE MORROW LINDBERGH

It was so quiet. I sat in my room, covered by the silence. I wondered if it was time to eat, but I didn't want to eat alone. I turned on the television, forty-eight channels and nothing to watch.

It was late Friday afternoon. I had just completed my hospitalization program and was due to start what was called PHP, the Partial Hospitalization Program. I was supposed to have left the hospital soon after lunch, but I had stayed a little longer. For the next two weeks I was to stay in a local hotel and return to the hospital from 8:00 A.M. to 5:00 P.M., Monday through Friday.

I sat around in the patient lounge nursing a cup of coffee. I talked to one of the nurses for a while and discovered that she too had been a patient in this very unit a couple of years before. I felt as if she were giving me a gift by disclosing that she had walked where I was walking. I wandered back to my room to pack my suitcase. An older nurse came in and returned all my personal items. I looked at the hair dryer and smiled to myself at being once again trusted with this "lethal" weapon. The nurse asked if I had any suicidal thoughts. I replied that I did not. I walked into the lobby to reclaim my car keys. As I waited for the desk nurse to unlock her drawer, I looked around. I remembered that first night and the fear I had felt in being there; now I was afraid to leave.

As I looked out the hotel window to the traffic below, I wondered where all the people were going. It was dark even though it was still quite early, and the traffic was bumper to bumper. Washington, D.C., was committed to getting home from work.

I decided I would feel better if I was a part of the sea of life outside my door, so I picked up my jacket and walked to the elevator. I wondered if I looked strange. Would people waiting with me at the elevator whisper, "I think that she just got out of *that* hospital."

I went to the front desk and asked if there was a mall close at hand. The receptionist gave me directions, and I went out to my car. Once again I thought of how familiar the hospital had become to me; I felt safe there. My mother would arrive from Scotland in a couple of days, but for now—for a weekend—I was on my own.

I didn't know anyone in Washington, and I had not told anyone in Virginia that I was "out." I had not, in fact, talked to anyone at "The 700 Club" since I had left. I felt very vulnerable. One of the women in my group was staying at the same hotel, but she had plans to be with friends that first night and I did not want to "gate crash" her time.

I parked as close to the busy mall as I could and wandered in. People seemed to be falling over each other to get to where they wanted to be. I bought a cup of *real* coffee from a gourmet store; no more decaffeinated for me. I was back in the big world, and I needed it fully leaded. I sat and watched the men, women, and children who scurried past me: frustrated husbands who found themselves engulfed once more in a shopping frenzy; children who wanted to stop and take in the full joy of some novelty that caught their eye but who were hurried on by their parents. Suddenly, I felt painfully alone. I looked into the eyes of a woman who seemed to be carrying the weight of the world on her shoulders. I wondered about her life, and was saying a quiet prayer for her when I realized someone was talking to me.

"Sheila, we are so pleased to see you. We have been praying for you."

I looked up at a woman in her forties, who was smiling as she talked.

"This is my husband, Bill, and we watch 'The 700 Club' every day, don't we, Bill?" Bill agreed. "How are you, dear?" she asked.

"I'm doing much better than I was a month ago," I said.

"We're so glad. We will keep you in our prayers and hope to see you back on the air in no time." She reached over and hugged me, and they were gone.

I found the nearest bathroom, locked myself in and cried. I didn't know why I was crying. I just felt more alone after they left. I wished I could have sat down and had dinner with them, to be with someone. I dried my eyes and decided to head back to the hotel. Being in the mall made me feel too lost in the crowd.

It was now dark and cold, and I didn't have the right clothes with me. I had packed in a numb stupor when I left Virginia Beach. What on earth had I been thinking about? I had packed summer dresses and T-shirts, as if I were heading off on a cruise instead of checking into a hospital.

I reached my car and pulled out of the mall entrance onto the highway. I was suddenly afraid, as if I had forgotten how to drive at night. All sorts of thoughts crashed in on me, and I pulled into a McDonald's parking lot to pull myself together. I love to drive, it is a passion of mine, but all the lights and the noise around me seemed dark and threatening. As I sat there with rain beginning to fall on my windshield, I reminded myself that I was not alone; God was with me. Even though I knew the words were true, I still felt cold inside.

Back in my motel room, I sat at the desk for a long time, with my Bible open, its pages staring up at me. I felt as if I were standing on the edge of a wasteland that stretched out endlessly before me. The last month had been spent in trying to find my balance again. But the journey was just beginning. I was coming to grips with the impact my father's death had had on my life, and I was beginning to understand the subsequent choices I had made, but where did that leave me now?

While I was grateful for the lessons I was learning, and, in a sense, the storm had passed, I now sat in the aftermath looking at the devastated landscape wondering what would become of my life. I knew that it could never be "business as usual" again. Even though I was touched by the kind and hopeful words of the couple in the mall who expected to see me back on the air very soon, I knew returning there would not be right for me or for "The 700 Club."

It seemed as if the road ahead were dark and lonely. I could not see how far it stretched; all I knew was that it was the only way home.

I slept late on Saturday morning and then watched old black-and-white movies on American Movie Classics. I didn't leave the room all day.

Sunday morning when I woke up, I decided I would go back to the church I had visited with the other patients the previous week. God had spoken powerfully to me there, and I wanted to hear his voice again. As I got dressed, I felt a surge of hope. It was normal to feel a little dissociated when you are released from a hospital, I told myself, particularly when you have been surrounded by a loving, caring staff— brothers and sisters in Christ.

In the sanctuary I sat in the same place as before, but I didn't see anyone I recognized. I had remembered the singing as being warm and strong; now it seemed lifeless. I listened hard to the pastor's sermon, trying in vain to hear God speak to me.

When the service was over, everyone filed out, heading off to a family lunch or home to watch a ball game. I stayed and sat for a while, looking at the beautiful stained glass windows. Last week the sunlight had danced through them; now they were dull and quiet.

As I walked to my car I felt chilled all over. I had nothing to do until eight o' clock the next morning, and I didn't want to go back to my room and spend the whole day there again, so I drove downtown to Union Station. I sat in a little cafe, watching the people walk by. I tried to ignore my thoughts, but they would not go away. *This is your life now, Sheila. This is how it will be.*

I felt as if the hospital had given me a false picture of what was real. Of course I felt loved there; that was their job. Of course they listened; they were paid to listen. But that time was coming to an end, and now I would be all alone.

Why had I felt nothing in church? Where was God? Perhaps it would be different now—because I would be of no use to him anymore. I knew he still loved me and that I would be with him one day in heaven, but for now he seemed far away. I thought again of all my lofty declarations of faithfulness to the Lord, of how I would never let him down, and how here I was, alone and silent. I had no idea what I would do. All of my life I had trained and prepared for only one thing, to serve God—that was my life.

Unable to think too far ahead, I sat in the Union Station coffee shop and prayed, asking the Lord to show me where I should go now.

OTHER TRAVELERS

> In the real dark night of the soul it is always three o'clock in the morning.
>
> F. Scott Fitzgerald, *The Crack-up*

The phrase "dark night of the soul" is the title of a beautiful work written by St. John of the Cross, a sixteenth-century church reformer who dedicated his life to calling people back to a life of obedience and prayer. He was regarded as a radical, was arrested and imprisoned, and yet the effort to silence him gave birth to his loudest and most enduring cry, for in prison he wrote *The Dark Night of the Soul*, in which he describes his experience of being led by God to a place where, in love, the Lord "wounds" him. Based on this experience, John of the Cross saw that God's divine plan leads us to a place where, through the pain of our broken lives, we are ready to change to become more like Christ. Imprisonment, for this reformer, wasn't the end of the road, but the beginning of his journey.

Many of the most inspiring books and illuminating lives have been born out of what we would call tragedies. The common thread woven throughout these stories is that, in the midst of their pain, the men and women reached for the hand of the Shepherd of their souls. Perhaps, like me, you can remember praying to be more like the Lord. But when life began to shake, it seemed as if you were losing ground rather than getting closer to heaven.

As I read through the pages of *The Dark Night of the Soul*, I was amazed at the places that made me stop and say, "Yes, that's right. That's exactly how I feel." To use the words of Charles Dickens, John was saying that this dark night was, for him, "the best of times" and "the worst of times." He talked of the pain and the loneliness that sat with him, and yet he was deeply aware that this was a place to which God had led him. Many different roads can lead to this same dark night. When you find yourself there, it does not matter what brought you to your knees, what matters is that you are there.

In hindsight, I believe that the way home for all pilgrims is through this bitter wasteland. It is there when all help and all hope is gone, that we finally learn to trust in the only One who can teach us how to live. We arrive at this rusted, uninviting gateway through many different circumstances—some out of our control and some that we have brought upon ourselves. But if our trust is in Christ, he will pilot us through the deepest valleys and we will never be the same again.

Of the Bible's countless examples of those who faced their own dark night and left a little light for us to see by, none is more poignant than the life of Christ. Christ had never needed his friends more than he did in Gethsemane, but they slept through his brow-bloodied prayers. His anguished cries to his Father pierced the night, but the world slept through his sorrow. He had no shoulder to cry on, no hand to hold, no one to comfort him. As he was nailed to a wooden cross at the place of the skull, he cried out the greatest fear of us all, "My God, my God, why have you forsaken me?" (Matthew 27:46).

Job is another example of a life turned upside down for no apparent reason. The darkness hit him with no warning. I used to find it so hard to understand why God would allow Satan to torment a man like Job. He lived a good life, not just a casually good life, but a life committed to honoring God. He lived with acute intentionality. "This man was blameless and upright; he feared God and shunned evil" (Job 1:1).

Surely, it is the whole point of our lives to fear God and to honor him, but God wanted something more from Job. In one day, he lost everything. Job's response to this catastrophe was, "The LORD gave and the LORD has taken away; may the name of the LORD be praised" (Job 1:21).

But Job's troubles were not yet over. He then broke out in sores from the top of his head to the soles of his feet. His wife asked him why he did not curse God and die. Job responded that we cannot accept good from God and not trouble.

When the dust had settled in Job's life, as is true with anyone, the real battle was just beginning. For a short time after tragedy strikes, we are borne along by the pace of events. When the volcano is in full force, it is an awesome sight. But when the lava dries and the white ash settles, it is deathly still. The cold, gray blanket of winter settled onto Job's shoulders.

When you look at the response of Job's friends, it's amazing to see how little has actually changed over the years. They had no idea what Job was experiencing. The only thing they brought to their suffering friend was words, which they tossed his way to see if any would stick. Their impatience with him is obvious; he was disturbing the quiet of their waters, and they wanted life to be back to normal as soon as possible.

Before I was admitted to the hospital, I cleared my calendar of any commitments in the months ahead. I was booked to sing and speak at a women's conference nine months away; I called the woman in charge and told her I was very sorry, but I would not be able to come. She was very upset. I apologized for any inconvenience I was causing and offered to refund any money she had already spent on promotion. Apparently, that wasn't the problem; she just wanted me to come. I tried to explain what was happening to me—that I was being admitted to the hospital the next day. She answered, "You do not need to do that. I will pray for you now, and then you will be able to be with us and testify to the fact that God healed you."

She was just not hearing me. When confronted with an inconvenient situation that clashed with her theology, she wanted it to change. I was in such distress that I couldn't think of what to say to her. She concluded by saying that she would make a few phone calls to see if I was telling the truth.

When someone is in pain and at the beginning of the longest night of their lives, an endless barrage of words like those from Job's friends and those I received from this woman is like thunder in the desert: a loud and comfortless noise.

Probably the most damaging counsel offered to Job came from the young man Elihu. He basically told Job that his life made no difference. He pointed out that God is God, Job was a man. Whatever happened in life happened, and there was nothing they could do. He attacked Job's commitment to integrity in the midst of his battle, saying, "If you sin, how does that affect him [God]? ... If your sins are many, what does that do to him? If you are righteous, what do you give to him?" (Job 35:6–7).

Elihu said there was no purpose in all of Job's suffering. I imagine most of us in times of crisis have encountered similar friends or are haunted by similar doubts and fears, but we need to hold on beyond such skeptical visitors, because after they have had their say, the Lord speaks. For Job, God pulled back the curtain for a moment and gave him a glimpse of who God is. All Job could say was, "My ears had heard of you but now my eyes have seen you" (Job 42:5).

This simple statement is one of the most profound in the entire canon of Scripture. It lays out the vast difference between head knowledge and heart knowledge. I have been a student of the Bible since I was a young girl, but now I read it differently. When I was a child, I committed verses of Scripture to memory, so I could carry one more Bible prize home to my mother. When I sat at my desk at CBN answering correspondence, I would scan the pages to find a verse that seemed to fit each letter I received. But now I knew that the words that were life to me, my bread and water and air were: "I know that my Redeemer lives, and that in the end he will stand upon the earth" (Job 19:25).

Even as I reread the story of Job during the weeks that followed, I still found myself asking "why." I know that Job's story has a happy ending, but the cost attached to the lesson he learned was immense. I thought of my friend Debbie, who had been struggling for so long with cancer and was now in constant pain. What could I say to her? I did not feel that I could tell her, "Hang in there. It gets better in the end."

I felt as if I were a child again, starting at the very beginning, asking the most basic questions: "What is the purpose of my life? How do I walk in the will of God? How do I live in a way that makes God happy? What does God want of me? What does it *look* like to be a Christian?"

As I entered this new phase of treatment—and of life— God was painfully silent. When I prayed, I understood what people meant when they said it seemed their prayers went no higher than the bedroom ceiling. Still, I kept praying, and I kept reading the psalms out loud; it was all I knew to do. David had walked this path before me and had experienced the absence of God. His prayer became my prayer. I prayed out my loneliness. I prayed out my fear and anger. I prayed out the agony of being a fragile, flawed human being.

DARK NIGHT EXPOSES SIN

In *The Dark Night of the Soul*, John of the Cross clearly lays out what he believes to be God's purpose in turning out the lights. It is to expose our sin, including the following elements of sin, which I saw in my own life.

Pride. John of the Cross talks about the initial "heady" days of faith, when we are overwhelmed with the love of God and passionately committed to sharing that with others. There is, he says, a tendency to judge other people and elevate oneself in the secret places of the heart. I identify with that indictment; I remember those days well. I used to love it when people would tell me that I had a remarkable ministry. While that kind of comment should have brought me to my knees before God, it just made me feel a little more invincible. At times I had longed to get help for my life, but the price was too high; I too highly valued the respect and recognition I was given. It was as if I had a compulsion to teach and an unwillingness to be taught. Insidious pride disguises itself to look admirable on the outside, while inside, a little worm begins to grow.

Spiritual greed. Like an addict who craves a bigger and better high, the believer craves more intense religious feelings. It is wonderful to feel the presence of the Lord, but our commitment needs to be out of obedience to him, rather than because it makes us feel good. When we live our lives as if God exists for us—to make us happy—we have missed the point completely. Our childish behavior is based on emotional thrills. What does that self-indulgent euphoria have to do with Calvary? The whole purpose of our lives is to glorify God, to say with every fiber of our beings that we exist for him.

When I felt my life starting to shake, I looked for some *experience* that would deliver me from my trouble. I crammed my mind with books and tapes in a frantic search of a touch from heaven. I never thought to stop all my *doing* and listen. John says that out of love for his children, God will take our lives and purge them in the dark fire.

Richard Foster writes, "For a soul will never grow until it is able to let go of the tight grasp that it has on God." This almost sounds blasphemous, and yet I understand a little of what he means. So often we cling more to our theory of who God is than to who he really is as he has revealed himself in Christ and through his Word. I am grateful for the wonderful books available to help us in our walk with God, but too often they take the place of God's Word; we ingest the opinions and experiences of men or women who no doubt love the Lord, but whose words should never take the place of scriptural revelation. No matter how gifted any of us are as communicators, we are all followers, all servants, all seekers, and God is the only truth on which we can stake our lives. We are told to make our requests known to God, to ask and keep on asking, but we should always ask in an attitude of humility and awe, not demanding that he live up to our feel-good television commercials.

Anger and disillusionment. As we face the sin of our spiritual greed, we are often confronted with anger toward and our disillusionment with God. Often, when God calls us to "grow up" as Christians, we respond like petulant children who do not want to be weaned from their mother's breast. When it seems as if God has left us and no longer answers our prayers, we may become angry and disillusioned. John of the Cross says this frustration with our situation is not true humility, which waits for God, demanding nothing, surrendering the desire to become a "saint in a day."

Over the years I have received many letters from Christians who are disappointed in God. A lot of teaching presents God as a benevolent sugar daddy in the sky, and when our lists of requests do not materialize, we become angry with him as if he had failed to live up to some agreement that we ourselves dreamed up. It requires little faith or commitment to follow someone who sits with a magic wand, awaiting our bidding. That is not who God is. When prayer no longer brings feelings of heaven, when God's Word stares silently from the page, the disillusioned disciple walks away like a disappointed fan whose team is in a slump.

DARK NIGHT AND SURRENDER

God in his mercy, out of a desire for a real relationship with us, will continue to allow us to fall flat on our faces until all we want is him. He is so committed to our spiritual health and growth that he will do whatever it takes to free us from our selfish nature. But this is no mindless, barbaric endurance test. He knows us well and loves us lavishly.

God's purposes are for our good, never for our destruction. We have the comfort of knowing that God, who created us, who knew us before we were born, and who perfectly knows us, has promised us that he will not permit us to be given more than we can bear. "He will not let you be tempted beyond what you can bear.... he will also provide a way out so that you can stand up under it" (1 Corinthians 10:13).

This is a concrete promise: At the right time God will say, "It is enough." In the midst of the most painful times, I really wondered if that verse were true. I honestly believed what was happening to me *was* more than I could bear, and I wondered if God had forgotten me. It seemed that if one more thing was laid on my back—even a feather—I would break. But our God is good. As C. S. Lewis said in *The Lion, the Witch and the Wardrobe*, our Lion-King is not necessarily *safe*, but he is good.

In the dark night when no one is watching, we are given the opportunity to face ourselves and surrender wholly to Christ. I have heard many sermons on the subject of surrender; I have sung many songs that speak of little else. But what does it really mean? For me, it meant walking away from everything I loved, because I had lost touch with Jesus, the One whom I am called to love.

I had to come to a point of asking myself, "Does God exist for me or do I exist for him?" The answer was and is very clear. I exist to love and serve God. He does not owe me a thing, but I owe him everything.

One of the most inspiring works I have ever read is *The Imitation of Christ* by Thomas à Kempis. Although he completed this book in 1427, the wisdom and humility displayed within its pages are utterly relevant to life today. Referring to the times in our lives when everything is dark, when there is a desolation of spirit, he says:

> It is no great thing to despise the comfort of man, when the comfort of God is present. But it is a great thing and indeed a very great thing, that a man should be so strong in spirit as to bear the lack of both comforts and for the love of God and for God's honor should have a ready will to bear desolation of spirit and yet in nothing to seek himself or his own merits.

During this dark time I saw how strong my will is. I like to be in control; I feel too vulnerable if I am not calling the shots. But now I found myself in a place where obedience—not what made me feel good—was all that mattered. As I read *The Imitation of Christ*, I saw that it was not for me to question what God was doing in my life or how long that process would take. In my younger years, it had been relatively easy for me to fast for extended periods of time or to pray and work intensely with great self-discipline. Now I saw that God

119

wanted my heart and mind as well as a focused vision. It is spiritual suicide to throw oneself into the work of God, only to forget the face of God. Step by step, I surrendered the tight hold that I had had on my life for so long.

As I continued as an outpatient at the hospital, it became clearer to me that fear made me clench my fists. I sat in sessions with my therapist and listened as my mother talked about her own dark night. She described the darkest night of her journey, when it seemed as if the very powers of hell came into her bedroom to torment her. All sorts of sickening thoughts tore through her mind as she faced the reality of losing the man she loved and of raising three children by herself. In the midst of this attack, one "dart" bounced off her shield of faith. The voice said to her, "You are all alone in the world tonight. No one is praying for you."

My mother knew that could not be true. She knew that her grandmother, a great saint of God, would never have gone to sleep without getting down on her knees on her granddaughter's behalf.

As I sat and listened, I saw my mother's faith rise again, even as she told her story. I realized that in the midst of the worst agony of her life, she did not forget who she was. Her identity as a child of God, descended from a long line of godly people, charted her through the pitch dark of night.

One evening we sat in a restaurant and talked about the future. I had no idea what to do. Everything I had been involved in for the previous ten or twelve years revolved around a stage, and I did not believe that long-term healing could occur in a spotlight. Surface wounds heal quickly, but deeper wounds take time. So much of my life had been built around my career, and now that landscape seemed decimated.

That evening, with tears running down my cheeks, I prayed a very simple but life-changing prayer: "Father, I stand before you now with empty hands. Whatever you put in my hands, I will welcome and whatever you take away, I will gladly let it go."

The first step—the prayer—was relatively easy. Walking it out daily is what would prove difficult. When I fail, I am grateful for the mercy and forgiveness of God. And I am learning that because I am so strong willed, it is important for me to surrender to God without a barrage of questions—to *choose* to obey as an act of will.

C. S. Lewis describes surrendering ourselves to God as the difference between looking *along* a beam of light and looking *into* a beam of light. In a book of essays titled *God in the Dock*, he describes this experience as it happened to him while sitting in a toolshed. He was watching a shaft of sunlight pouring through a crack in the wood. It was the only thing that he could see—everything else was dark— until he stood up and looked through the beam. Then, everything was changed; he could not see the beam at all, and yet the scene outside the woodshed was illuminated.

We can choose to live in the darkness, observing life from the safety of the sidelines, or we can step into the light and be given a bigger vision. Lewis faced his own time of agony and despair. The movie *Shadowlands* portrays something of that path of broken glass Lewis was to walk upon in the latter years of his life. He was a brilliant writer and apologist who spoke eloquently on many issues of faith, but his own taste of suffering changed his paradigm forever. In the movie we see him standing at a lectern giving a masterly speech on the purpose of suffering. The delivery was brilliant, but detached.

Then Lewis lost his wife to cancer. In the midst of his pain, it seemed to him that God was not listening, as if a door was slammed in his face "and all that I could hear was the sound of bolting and double bolting." In time he spoke as one who had walked through the valley of the shadow of death. It seems as if that is the way: At first there is the cry in the darkness, "My God, my God, why have you forsaken me?"

Lewis called pain "God's megaphone": Rather than being evidence that God does not care, pain is overwhelming evidence that he does. When Lewis looked *along* the beam of suffering, he spoke with eloquence. After he had stood in the place of suffering and the beam had hit him, he spoke with compassion and grace.

I recently read an interesting modern parable that spoke to this issue of darkness as a teacher. In his book, *Healing the Shame That Binds You*, John Bradshaw tells of a man who was sentenced to die and placed in a dark cave. He was told that there was a way out, and if he could find it in thirty days, he would be free. High above him, there was a small hole through which food was lowered to him every day. The man spent every waking moment trying to build a pile of stones high enough to climb to the top, to that tiny shaft of light, but by the time that he was close to the opening he was exhausted from his efforts and fell to his death.

If the prisoner had only known that one of the stones in the side of the cave, about two hundred feet from him, had been pushed away, he could have escaped with little difficulty. Bradshaw concludes: "He had so completely focused on the opening of light, that it never occurred to him to look for his freedom in the darkness."

It takes time to hear God in the darkness. It will take quiet, and quiet is a gift. "In repentance and rest is your salvation, in quietness and trust is your strength" (Isaiah 30:15). None of us would seek pain in our lives, but when you find yourself in a bleak place, it is time to pay attention to what God would say to you in the darkness. You might be surprised by what he will show you about your life. I know I was.

> *It is dark, Lord.*
> *I feel so alone.*
> *I am like a boat that is lost at sea.*
> *I know that you are with me;*
> *chart me through this long, dark night.*
> *Amen.*

＄

You hold the scales of justice
so tightly to your chest;
I wish you'd lay them down
and let me rest there on your breast.

＄

8
Forgiveness Comes Full Circle

Be kind and compassionate to one another,
forgiving each other,
just as in Christ God forgave you.

Ephesians 4:32

Let me describe for you my idea of a perfect evening. It's cold outside, possibly raining. A hearty fire is burning in the fireplace. It crackles and dances and sings. Abigail, my cat, is stretched out, purring generously, her cream fur orange in the flame's glow.

Friends have come over and we've had a meal that we threw together at the last moment and somehow turned out to be just right, and now we sit as close to the fire as Abigail will allow and tell stories—stories of our lives, stories we were told as children, stories born in our imaginations.

Few things are more glorious to me than storytelling. My mother has always been an avid reader. She chose to leave school when she was fifteen to help her mother with my grandfather who was ill, but her education continued through the pages of Charles Dickens and A. J. Cronin. We grew up in a small town, but in a huge world through the gift of stories. I had more than a few favorites.

I've already told you of *The Wizard of Oz* and *The Velveteen Rabbit.* And then there was *Beauty and the Beast,* which had all the "right" elements, including a lonely, beautiful heroine who faced terrible danger. Yet in the midst of this heroine's fear, she reached out to the beast, who was transformed by the power of her love.

The Ugly Duckling told a different, yet similar tale. In this story, a lonely little fellow, misunderstood by others, is finally transformed into the most beautiful swan of all. Those who had rejected him are the very ones to tell him, once he becomes a swan, how magnificent he is.

The very premise of a fairy tale is that all wrongs will be righted, that good will triumph over evil, and that, in the end, truth will be revealed and the story will come full circle. It all happens within a few pages, and it all happens on this earth.

But we do not live in Hans Christian Andersen's world. We live in this world. As Christians, we know there will come a day when all tears will be wiped away, when peace and joy will be the only songs we know, but we have a long road to walk until that Day of the Lord. For the moment, we have to live with one another, with all the good and bad that comes with it. The sad truth is that we will let one another down. We will fail. We will bruise each other. So how should we live in the midst of this reality?

In the previous chapter, I talked about the first days after my release from the hospital. Now I'd like to walk you through four lessons I learned on the road to forgiveness. This road carried me back to Virginia Beach at the end of my Washington program, but the lessons started when I was in the hospital, well before my PHP days. Actually, the lessons started years before my breakdown.

SOWING AND REAPING

When we find flaws, we find it hard to walk with one another for the duration of the journey. Too often we leave a trail of bodies behind us. I think of situations when friends of mine were in trouble and I believed it was my duty to them and to the Lord to help pull them up by their boot-straps. Based on what appeared to be happening on the out-side, I made some quick judgment calls.

If someone lets us down, we walk away. This hap-pened to me. What was most painful was that I knew I had done the very same thing to a friend when she needed me. She was one of my few good friends. We went on trips together, sat for hours talking over endless cups of coffee. We laughed and cried as we shared our hopes and dreams for the future. Then one day she sat me down and told me that she thought she was gay. My first question was, "Does your husband know?"

Yes, he did. I was absolutely stunned. I had naively assumed that this issue never reared its head among Chris-tians. My friend was taking a risk telling me, reaching out to me for some kind of support—not endorsement, but a sign that I was still her friend.

And when she needed me most, I was not there. All I could think of was *she must be telling me because she is interested in pursuing that kind of a relationship with me.* I ran for miles. She was a friend in trouble, and I aban-doned her.

Now, years later, I sat in the doctor's office in the hos-pital with tears rolling down *my* cheeks. I felt crushed and thrown away.

"What is on your mind, Sheila?" he asked.

"I thought these people were my friends," I said. The people I was speaking of were those who had just walked away from me when my life had started to unravel. They were the people who had put an unsympathetic twist on my "breakdown." Was Satan really using me to attack CBN? Was "heaven" really "not pleased with me"?

Once I entered the hospital, more rumors had begun flying. The evangelical world is a fairly small place, and news, especially bad news, travels fast. Bits and pieces of these rumors had been getting back to me, and I was stunned by them. All of them were untrue: from "she's had an affair" to "she's been hallucinating and seeing flying things." And some people—friends—were believing these stories without even talking to me.

"I can't believe some of the things that are being said about me. It makes me wonder if we were ever friends at all."

I was angry and I was hurt, but I did not know what to do. I knew that God had brought me to the hospital to give me an opportunity to look at my life and make some changes. It was hard enough dealing with what was true without trying to extinguish false fires.

The doctor said, "Why don't you go back to your room and talk to the Lord about this. Write out how you feel."

I sat down at my desk very angry. I wrote down the names of the people who had most hurt me. As I sat there, another name came to mind: the friend I had walked away from. I tried to push that thought away; that was not the point of today's exercise, or so I thought. But it became very clear to me that my reaction to her was *exactly* the point. I tried to reason it away—our circumstances were so different—but the Holy Spirit would have none of that. The fact remained that I was now reaping in my own life what I had sown in another's life. Perhaps if I had been more gracious in the past when my friend had needed me, then I would be experiencing more grace in my own life when I needed it so badly.

My friend needed to know, as she struggled with the sin and pain in her own life, that she had a companion in the journey. But I had refused to be there for her. As I allowed this realization to flood over me, I was horrified by what I had done. I wrote her a letter that day, telling her that I understood now what I had done to her. I asked for her for-giveness. I knew that she might not even acknowledge my letter, but I also knew that I had to do whatever it took to confess that I had seriously wronged her.

Within a few days, she wrote back to me, forgiving me for what I had done. Her letter was gracious and magnanimous. She truly forgave me. It was my first lesson in forgiveness.

EXTEND THE MERCY

A second lesson started to sink in on my second Sunday in Washington. That Sunday a group of about eight patients hopped in a van and attended church together. We sat on the right side of a beautiful, small church. Sunlight streamed through the stained glass, bringing it to life. The singing inspired me. It felt like a holy place.

When the pastor stood to give his message, I thought to myself that he looked as if he had weathered some storms of his own. I sat up and paid attention. He read Matthew 18:21–35, the story of the unmerciful servant. This man owed his master ten thousand talents, millions of dollars in U.S. currency. Wanting to settle all outstanding accounts, the master asked his servant to repay what he owed. When the man was unable to do so, the master decided to sell this servant and his wife and children as slaves to recoup some of his loss.

Well, the servant fell on his knees and begged for mercy. He asked for more time to make good on his loans. At this, the merciful master took pity on his servant. He didn't just grant his servant's request for more time; he forgave him the entire debt.

The servant left rejoicing, but soon ran into a man who owed *him* a few dollars. Showing no mercy, he demanded that this man pay up immediately. When the man was unable to do so, the servant had him thrown in jail.

But that's not the end of the story. When the master heard what his servant had done to someone who owed him so little, he threw the servant in jail too—until he could repay the millions he had owed.

Matthew concludes: "That is how my heavenly Father will treat each of you unless you forgive your brother from your heart" (Matthew 18:35).

The issue uppermost in my mind that morning was my own desperate need of God's mercy and forgiveness. But a few days later as I sat in my room, the rest of the story began to visit me. It was clear to me that God was saying, "I have forgiven you for so much. I have wiped all your sins away. Because of my Son's sacrifice, you are free. Now extend that mercy to others."

I did not want to do that. I was hurt and angry, and I wanted those who had hurt me to at least acknowledge they had done so—and ask to be forgiven. But the Lord would not let me rest. I was to forgive, and I was to forgive now. "How do I do this, Lord?" I prayed. "I will just be pretending, because I do not feel anything in my heart. It will only be words."

It still seemed that God was requiring something of me. It didn't matter if it made sense to me or if I felt like doing it. In obedience to this call, I began to write down the names of the people I was angry with. As I put some of those names on paper, I found myself weeping, thinking of former times when there had been peace between us—times when things had been very different.

I could write the names down. I could even think about forgiveness. But to actually forgive them—I did not know how to do it. For that, I needed a third lesson.

FORGIVENESS FACE-TO-FACE

The very next day I heard a lecture on forgiveness. As I looked around the room, I realized how much harder forgiveness must be for some of the other patients than for me. Some of these women had been sexually molested by family members. How do you begin to forgive that?

Another of the women had been brutally beaten by her husband. What did forgiveness mean for her? She stood up and told the group that she could not forgive. It would mean everything that had happened to her was forgotten, and she could not afford to forget. The doctor told her four things:

Forgiveness does not minimize what has been done
to you.
Forgiveness does not make the pain go away.
Forgiveness does not blot out your memory.
Forgiveness is a God-given strategy for dealing with
the pain of life.

As I further processed what was happening in my life,
I discovered a substantial stumbling block to my forgiving
others: I found it very hard to forgive myself, so when I
encountered judgment in others it only served to reinforce
what I already believed about myself.

This started even before I left Virginia Beach. There
came a point when people did not stop by my office the way
they had before. I was definitely no longer the "flavor of the
month," as the saying goes. The staff seemed kind, but distant.
I was not myself. I was quiet and thin. I cried too much or
laughed too loudly. It was clear to people that something was
happening in my life, and it was not clear exactly how it would
play out, so friends to whom I had been close kept away.

I felt such an overwhelming burden of failure. I had
promised God that he could always count on me, and now I
could barely function. I felt like one of those star acts at the
circus. People had once applauded me and watched me
with fascination, but now that I had lost my grasp of the
trapeze bar, everyone stood back in horror, watching me fall
from the sky. In my final days at CBN, no one seemed to
know what to do.

I was wounded and utterly frustrated by letters I
received from friends before I entered the hospital, telling
me to "get your act together," and insisting that what was
happening to me was "not pleasing to the Lord." How can
someone stand in front of an erupting volcano and tell the
volcano, "Don't do this"? The letters made me realize how
conditional many of my relationships were. The clear message was, if you pull yourself together in a way that makes
sense to us, we will continue to be your friends. If not, we

will have to walk away. I began to see how I had set myself up for this response. I had been so passionately committed to being the perfect Christian since I was a young girl that "perfect Christian" was the only Sheila Walsh many people knew. If she was no longer there, the new Sheila was a stranger.

After I finished the PHP program, I went back to Virginia to find out what the next step should be. I was going to meet with Pat Robertson to talk about my future with CBN. Terry Meeuwsen, who used to fill in for me when I was on vacation, had been taking my place temporarily until a final decision was made. As I thought and prayed about the future, a new seed began to grow in me. I had spent so many years being the one who was supposed to have all the answers; now I wanted to be the one who was learning and growing. The seed grew rapidly, and I made tentative inquiries about going to seminary. By the time I sat down with Pat a week later, I had been provisionally accepted at Fuller Theological Seminary. He was excited for me and agreed that a couple of years away from the pressures of public life would be a wise decision.

One of my coworkers at "The 700 Club" called me a few days later and told me that a reporter from the *National Enquirer* was on my tail, trying to get a photograph of me drooling or talking to ducks. I could imagine the headline: "FORMER CO-HOST OF 700 CLUB SEEN ON BEACH IN BATHROBE TRYING TO WALK ON WATER."

The producer of "The 700 Club" asked me to appear on the next week's show as a guest. Viewers wanted to know what had happened to me, and the *Enquirer* would be less likely to run a story if I appeared on television looking relatively normal. (The story never ran.)

There was some debate as to whether I should tell viewers that I had been in a psychiatric hospital, but for me it was a moot point. That was the simple truth, and I needed to keep telling the truth as best I could.

I was extremely nervous as I drove through the CBN gates that morning in late November. I had done this same routine for years, but today was very different. I went upstairs to makeup. Terry Meeuwsen, the woman replacing me, was in my old dressing room. I stood at the door and took a deep breath. As I walked in, the two makeup artists came over to hug me, both with tears in their eyes. It was good to see them, and they set to work. When they were finished with me, I looked at myself in the mirror and thought, *Well, if the nurse who took away my makeup could see me now!*

I walked up the familiar steps to "The 700 Club" offices and along the corridor where my colleagues had their office spaces. One after the other, they came out to hug me and tell me they had missed me. It felt so healing to be there with them, and the forgiveness that had seemed cold on paper came to life face-to-face.

It was time to tape, so I went down to the studio. All the camera guys were there, including the floor director who had rescued me from many tough on-air situations (like the bear trainer who thought it would be easier to talk to me if he had his hand on my leg!). It was so good to see them all again.

I had prayed that morning that God would help me thank the viewers who had faithfully prayed for me—without losing it on the air. Pat Robertson was there and Ben Kinchlow and Terry. It felt strange to be the one being interviewed, and yet I was very aware of the Lord's presence as I sat in that chair. I thanked Pat for his love and support. I thanked those who had prayed and told them a little of what had happened to me. I told the audience that I had been praying for some time that God would show me what the next step was, and that I was going back to school for a master's in theology from Fuller Theological Seminary in California. I relayed how excited I was about this opportunity to go back to the basics of my faith and to listen and learn and grow.

After I had finished speaking, Pat prayed for me, and it was all over. I left the set. I decided I liked Terry a lot and, as I've subsequently watched her, I've come to admire her abilities as a journalist.

Before I left the building, one of the girls I had been closest to asked to talk to me. We sat on a window ledge in the corridor. She told me she was sorry she had not been there for me; she just hadn't known what to do. How well I understood that! As we hugged and said good-bye, it was clear to us that God was working in both our lives, teaching us what it meant to love God and each other.

I drove out of the main gates and prayed a blessing on this place in which I had learned so much. It was strange to say good-bye when it had been my whole life for so long. When I left for Washington, I had been afraid I would not be able to return, but now I was leaving freely and willingly. I left the grounds of CBN with a deeper appreciation for the gift of forgiveness that liberates all those who receive it and extend it to others, face-to-face.

In the month that followed that final appearance, I received and read more than five thousand letters from viewers telling me about their own stories. I was amazed at what I read. Letter after letter told of people struggling with their own depression or that of a loved one. I had no desire to become the poster child for depression, but I am glad that my last appearance on "The 700 Club" gave some people the courage to tell their own stories. As for myself, I was beginning a new journey.

UNBOUND!

The Lord showed me a fourth lesson in forgiveness. Before I left Virginia Beach, I went with a colleague to the ballet. It was a modern production, which is not usually my taste, but it had a profound impact on me. The opening dance was a depiction of a mother giving birth to her son. The dancer representing the baby stood wrapped in white cloth bandages. Other dancers began to unwrap them until the child was standing alone with one last sheath of cloth around his body. (I sense I'm losing some of you at this point!) The boy stood there, still convinced that he was confined. Then he realized that if he took a single step, the rest of the cloths would fall away. (Fortunately he did have tights on underneath!) As I watched this performance, I had an overwhelming sense of the Lord's saying: "Sheila, you are free. I brought some people into your life to start the process, but now you must walk in it."

As I began to forgive others, they returned to normal size. I no longer saw them in monster-like proportions. As long as I viewed someone as the enemy, I gave that person some power over my life. But as I forgave a person, I too was free. I saw that I could spend a lot of time imprisoned by past failures, or I could thank God for his never-ending grace and forgiveness and get on with the rest of my life.

This took me back to the lesson from Jesus' parable of the unmerciful servant. I had been forgiven much—and I was to continue to reach out to others with the grace God had offered me.

WALKING IN FORGIVENESS

> Here is a mental treatment guaranteed to cure every ill that man is heir to: Sit for half an hour every night and forgive anyone against whom you have any ill will.
>
> CHARLES FILLMORE, QUOTED IN
> *HOW TO HEAL DEPRESSION* BY HAROLD BLOOMFIELD

Before moving to Los Angeles, I continued to live in Virginia for a couple of months after coming back from the hospital. During that time, I met regularly with a wise and godly counselor who constantly urged me to ask myself in every situation, "What would Jesus do?"

This counselor helped me to work through the process of responding to broken relationships. Through all the pain and confusion, I learned that everything comes to me through the merciful and loving hands of God. Knowing this seemed to shift everything, to throw open the doorway between my past and my future. I thought of the story of Joseph. When he finally revealed to his brothers that he—the governor of Egypt—was the kid brother they had sold into slavery, they feared for their lives. Joseph told them not to be afraid; what they had intended for evil, God meant for good.

Joseph was an innocent man who had been seriously wronged, and his story has relevance for us all. If we have committed our lives into God's hands, we can trust him that even the worst storms will be used to make us more like Christ. This was the paradigm through which everything else in my life began to fall into place and make sense. The next steps were more difficult, but I knew now where to walk.

One of the most important steps for me was to allow anyone who felt disappointed or personally wounded by me to talk to me. My natural instinct is to stay away from what might be painful, to write people off and move on, but that is never the way of the Cross. I lived that way for too long, and it is the way of the coward. I want to deal with life honestly, seeking restoration wherever possible. I used to believe that pain was a negative force that would destroy me. I do not believe that anymore.

One of the hardest things I did was to talk to a man who had hurt me through his letter, which I received just before I went into the hospital. As I drove to his home, my heart pounded in my chest. We were both a little guarded at first as we sat at his kitchen table, drinking coffee. I told him I had wanted to see him because I knew he was angry with me and I wanted to give him an opportunity to say what he had to say face-to-face. I listened as he spoke about the confusion he experienced, as he described how helpless he felt to do anything. I told him that his letter had hurt me, but I was sorry for the pain I had caused. We only spent a couple of hours together, but the chasm between us was gone. We are friends to this day.

I accepted all those who were disappointed in me and gave them space to feel angry and wounded—even to walk away. If I knew someone had something against me, I went to them and asked them to say what was on their hearts. In each case, I tried not to be defensive but to really listen and ask for forgiveness where there was a wound.

In one instance, I had hurt someone through a careless remark and knew that I had to ask for forgiveness. I hardly knew the person but had heard through the grapevine that he was angry with me. I called his secretary and asked if he would see me. We arranged a meeting for the next day. As I rode the elevator to his office, I had no idea how the meeting would go. I only knew that I had an apology to make.

I sat in a busy reception area as people rushed in and out of a maze of offices. The man came to meet me and asked me to follow him. He sat quietly, waiting for me to begin. I told him I had come to ask for forgiveness. All sorts of excuses rumbled around in my mind, but none of them warranted utterance. I had wronged another human being, and that was all that mattered. The man was more than gracious and warmly accepted my apology. Minutes later I rode down the elevator, a humbled, grateful woman.

Whenever names or faces would come to mind and I felt some of the old resentment stirring, I would immediately begin to pray for those people, that God's blessing would be upon them.

What happened in the weeks and months that followed was an incredible learning experience for me. Some of those people are no longer in my life, and I have had to take time to grieve over that, accept it, and move on. The best gift of all, however, is that with those who continued to walk with me, no matter how rocky it got for a while, I have a depth of friendship that I never before knew was possible.

A FAITHFUL STORY

> I am convinced that nine out of ten people seeing a psychiatrist, do not need one. They need someone who will love them with God's love and then, they will get well.
>
> PAUL TOURNIER, *GUILT AND GRACE*

I have a story to tell that is far more wonderful to me than all the stories I have tucked away in my mind for a rainy day, because it happened to me. When I was at my lowest point, I had a friend who chose not to leave me, who refused to let go of me even when I was at my worst. We had worked together before I started at "The 700 Club." He had been part of the team that managed my career, but we had not seen each other in some time.

This person heard I was in trouble before I went into the hospital and tried to contact me, but I did not return his calls. At the time, I felt I was beyond help and could see no purpose in letting someone try.

He faxed me while I was in the hospital, but I ignored the faxes. Even so, he and his wife decided they would not give up on me. And when I was back in Virginia Beach after I left the hospital, he flew in from Nashville to tell me just that.

I remember sitting in a restaurant with him the day after I was released from the hospital. He spoke very succinctly: "You need friends right now, and we are here."

During the next few weeks and months, I went through all sorts of changes. Old fears rose to the surface. I wanted to give up, but he would not let me. Not once did he try to make light of what was happening to me or gloss over my responsibilities. He spoke the truth strongly to me, wrapped in a blanket of assurance that he and his wife were with me for the rest of the journey. He was committed to continuing the process that began in the hospital no matter how long it took.

I will never be able to adequately thank this friend and his wife for the gift they gave to me. Without them I doubt I would be standing where I am today—in peace and rest.

That kind of friendship is what the Lord intends for us all to have. That's the way it was supposed to be.

A PLEA FOR UNDERSTANDING

Much of this chapter on forgiveness has focused on my journey of mending broken relationships—of forgiving those who had caused me great pain and of asking forgiveness from those I had hurt.

I end this chapter with another true story, this one from another century. It is a story that teaches a lesson of forgiveness. This time, I will tell you the moral of the story before I begin: Many of the judgments we make of one another—judgments that cause great pain—are preventable, because they are based on misunderstanding and misinformation.

This story came to life for me while I was in the seminary during a course in church history. It was wonderful to be back in a classroom, to be surrounded by people who wanted to learn and grow. By the third semester, we had moved to recent history. For my finals, I chose to write a paper on covenant theology and the Salem witch trials. What happened in that little Massachusetts town in 1692 should never be forgotten.

Salem was a Puritan community that lived under a "covenant of works" and a "covenant of grace." This covenant of grace became a noose around the neck of many believers. Being accused of a sin was tantamount to being separated from Christian fellowship. If you confessed to the sin you were accused of, you received the "grace" of being welcomed back into the community. If you did not confess, you were damned in the eyes of the church.

The dilemma at Salem was this: What did you do if you were accused of a sin that you did not commit? Did you lie and say you were guilty in order to be reinstated into fellowship? Or did you tell the truth, claim your innocence, and face banishment—earthly damnation? Quite obviously, great power lay in the hands of the accuser.

In Salem, when some parents felt their children were becoming apathetic in their faith, the community emphasized revivals. In the winter of 1692, the religious fervor was high.

At the same time as these revivals were occurring, a few of the young girls began to meet with the minister's slave, Tituba. A Carib Indian, Tituba regaled them with tales of magic and folklore. The enthralled girls began to exhibit strange behavior, fainting, and screaming. The pastor, afraid of displays of emotion, made them fast and pray to quiet their souls, but this only served to make them more excitable.

Then the hammer fell. The girls began to accuse several women in the community of witchcraft. (Why, no one knows.) The situation escalated until more than a hundred innocent women came under suspicion. The accused knew their options: Confess to a sin that they did not commit and be restored to the community, or truthfully deny the accusation and be executed. Between June 10 and September 22, nineteen men and women and two dogs were hanged for witchcraft. One man, Giles Corey, was pressed to death between rocks. When given one last chance to save himself, he simply said, "More weight."

Twenty years later a court annulled the convictions, and all the girls who had accused the unfortunate victims admitted that their accusations had not been true. But twenty people were dead and families had been destroyed. Worse, they had been executed by people who loved God and who believed themselves to be the chosen remnant.

Today, our world is littered with broken, bitter people who need love and instead receive judgment. By love, I do not mean a soft, quiet thing, but a powerful force for good. Love breaks down and builds up. It is transforming. Judgment, however, brings condemnation and fear. It is cowardly because it distances itself from the pain of life. Rather than healing what is bent, it cripples and abandons.

True love, the love that speaks the truth and yet refuses to abandon others, gives people an opportunity to change. It even motivates them to change.

Perhaps God will bring someone to your mind as he did with me—someone who needs your love in the same way that Christ loved you. It is never too late to start again.

Dear Father, who forgives all our sins,
who showers us with mercy and compassion,
teach us to love as you love;
teach us to forgive as you forgive;
teach us to live as you lived.
For Christ's sake,
Amen.

Part 3
The Road Home

So many nights I sat alone
weighing the emptiness,
handling this stone.
Day after day, lost in the noise,
stifle the sadness, muffle the voice,
and then the hammer fell;
it took the house as well.
Let it go, let the whole thing go.

9
The Companionship of Brokenness

*Religion is for people who are afraid of going to hell.
Spirituality is for those who have been there.*

ROSS V.,
MEMBER OF A.A.

I'd been a patient in the hospital two weeks. It was Saturday, and on the weekends our daily schedule loosened up a bit. On Saturdays we could "play."

The sun decided to battle the November chill and bless us with a gloriously warm day. The staff encouraged us to vote on what we would do. Some of the younger women wanted to go shopping. Others voted for the Smithsonian. I cast my vote for an art exhibit of the works of several French impressionists. Two of the guys voted for a bait and tackle shop (which had about as much chance as my art exhibit!). We were stuck. We had to choose a place everyone would enjoy.

A staff member suggested we do something outdoors on such a pretty day, and we agreed. I suggested a picnic by the Potomac, but the bait and tackle guys were less than thrilled. Eventually we settled on a volleyball tournament. I was horrified. I've never been good at sports, especially when it comes to getting something over a net. I tried to dream up another idea, but it was no use. I was stuck. The days of doing whatever I wanted were over.

The decision made, I went to my room and grabbed a book, thinking I could read while the others played. It's hard to explain what it is like to be confined to a hospital for a time and then be taken on an outing. I have flown around the world, sung to royalty in the most beautiful theater in London, played to a capacity crowd at the Sydney Opera House, but none of those things gave me such joy as sitting in our little bus, heading off for a Saturday in the park.

I felt alive and free and happy—that is, until they put up the volleyball net. The bait and tackle guys, who were team captains, began to pick teams. When one of them called my name, I explained that I wasn't going to play; I would be reading. When the man insisted I be on his team, I replied that I did not know how to play and had as much desire to learn as I had to stick my hand in a blender. Then he told me not to be so selfish. I was shocked. *What does he mean?* I thought. *I'm doing him a favor!*

The man was obviously hurt by my unwillingness to risk looking like an idiot. I realized that I had not thought about how my decision would affect others—I was too aware of how it affected me. I hated to do things I was not good at and had always played to my strengths. Reluctantly, I agreed to join the game.

I would love to tell you that out there on that field I discovered the hidden athlete within me. I did not. I was actually worse than I thought I would be. If you never try something, you can hold onto the myth that you might be very gifted if you ever decided to give it your best shot. Out there on the field, I gave myself to it—and all myths were dispelled. As a volleyball player, I am truly awful. The funny thing is, I had a wonderful time. I had more fun that day, doing something that I was abysmal at, than I had during some of the most successful times in my life.

My team sized me up immediately and worked with me. I had no idea that it could be fun to do something you have no talent for, if you are doing it with people you care about and they too are having a good time. It was a very humbling lesson for me. Every time I would go for a shot and miss it by a mile, we would all laugh. My lack of ability seemed to bring me closer to people than my gifts ever had. I guess by that time I had nothing left to lose, no image to maintain. I was learning what it meant to be part of something, rather than being the whole show myself. After a while, I even got one over the net by myself. (It's just a pity the game was over by then!)

The next day the other patients voted me "entertainment secretary." My first act was to rent the movie *The Dream Team*, about a group of psychiatric patients who get lost on a field trip away from the hospital. I had seen it before and thought it funny, but it was much funnier to watch it with a bunch of psychiatric patients! We laughed so hard we could hardly breathe. I looked around the room at "Mary," who had been sexually abused by her father (who was coming in to talk to the doctors the next day), and at "Mike," who wore the scars of trying to take his own life. We were all laughing. We were laughing at ourselves, at the crazy things we do, at the ridiculous joy of life. Scripture tells us that laughter is as healing as any medicine: "A cheerful heart is good medicine, but a crushed spirit dries up the bones" (Proverbs 17:22). Of course, we still had to deal with the painful issues of our lives, but for a moment we allowed laughter to shake us just as surely as tears had.

On the next Saturday, we went bowling. One of the bait and tackle guys said that, to be fair, the other team should have me this time. I was a decided sports liability. Alas, I was as bad at bowling as I was at volleyball. If the object of the game had been to get the ball in the gutter, I would have been brilliant, but the rest of the players were unwilling to change the rules for me. They said I looked like Fred Flintstone when I was about to bowl, and that is not an image I care to cultivate.

Up until that point, I had always felt uncomfortable when people laughed at me; I viewed it as judgment and rejection. But when I started to laugh too, I saw that the laughter was a simple acknowledgment of my humanity. We were not laughing because I was a terrible person, but because I was a terrible bowler! I thought back to moments in my life when I had been unable to laugh, when I felt shamed by my failure. All sorts of pictures flashed before me.

I was twenty-two years old and working as an itinerant singer and speaker with Youth For Christ. One evening I was performing at a military camp in Germany. A thousand men and women filled the auditorium—an old building that needed some serious repair, as I was soon to discover. The camp commander introduced me. I walked on—and fell through a hole in the stage. The wood was rotting in places, and my right leg had found the perfect spot. There was a moment of quiet horror until, realizing I was unhurt, the audience began to roar with laughter. The whole thing must have been very funny—but I was dying inside. I felt like such a fool. I struggled through the concert, but couldn't wait for it to end. I had been given the perfect icebreaker, but, instead, it became an ice maker inside of me.

My thoughts moved on. Time after time I had withdrawn from people when I thought they perceived me as a failure. I always knew that my life encompassed joys and sorrows, successes and failures, moments of glory and moments of pain. And one reason I had led such a lonely life was to protect myself from the reaction I might get when the darker side of my life took center stage for a while. I protected myself from rejection by showing up only in situations where I could win. That is a very safe, but miserable place to live. Now I was learning to enjoy the companionship of brokenness.

Coming to terms with the reality of my own limitations as a human being was so liberating for me. I was reminded of the story of a Sunday school teacher who asked a student, "If good children are green and bad children are red, what color would you be, Mary?"

With the honesty of a child, she replied, "I'd be streaky."

That is the truth for my life. I am streaky. In fact, we are all streaky. One writer has said that there is a crack in every-thing God has made. This is not, however, a license to live in a careless way in hopes that our subsequent brokenness will teach us more about the grace and mercy of God. As Paul said, "What shall we say, then? Shall we go on sinning so that grace may increase? By no means!" (Romans 6:1–2). Instead, our weakness should lead us to deeper humility and greater dependency on God.

LONG ARMS, HIGH WALLS

The hospital program included an art class. I couldn't see any point in this at all. I have no talent for design and won-dered how this was supposed to be therapeutic. In one of our sessions, we were given a piece of clay and told to model a fig-ure that described our lives. I sat for a while, staring at this lump of clay. I did not know where to start. "Just do it, Sheila," the teacher said. "Don't think so much about it." I took the clay and began to mold. When I had finished, I was surprised by what I saw. I had made a little girl who lived inside a walled cir-cle. She looked like a normal girl except her arms were twice as long as they should have been.

"All right, class, you can stop now," the art therapist said. We were asked to walk around the room and look at one another's models, and then to say what we saw.

"Well, Sheila's is a giveaway!" someone said. "Arms long enough to reach out and help others, but no one gets to touch her." As I looked again, I saw it too: a wall that kept me safe, arms that made me useful—a lonely life.

LOVED TO LIFE

As I mentioned in connection with the shame profile, if you asked regular viewers of "The 700 Club," they might well say they knew a lot about me. If you suggested to them that I had a problem with intimacy, they may not have believed you. But there is a difference between bleeding all over people and sharing your true self at an appropriate level. To satisfy a deep desire for connection, I did all I knew how—I spilled myself over the camera. A healthier tack would have been to be totally open with God and myself and to have had an honest, vulnerable relationship with a few close friends. From that strong base of connectedness and security, I would have been able to be transparent with my audience out of the fullness of my life, not in a desperate attempt to connect with people whom I never saw face-to-face.

As each day in the hospital passed, I learned much from other patients about being vulnerable and transparent. At times, their honesty shocked me. They would voice their doubts and fears and allow others that same privilege. They seemed to gain strength by that very honesty; their faith was not diminished by their words, but honed and refined. I thought of the philosophy of Alcoholics Anonymous, where people introduce themselves in the most basic terms: "I'm Simon, and I'm an alcoholic." Surely that should be on our lips as the church: "I'm Sheila, and I'm a sinner."

Once I got out of the hospital, my doctor assured me, I would find new friends as long as I continued to be open and vulnerable. He was right. Everywhere I went, I found "real people"—who reminded me of the velveteen rabbit, loved-scrubbed to life. In my days of trying to be perfect, life had been all about me. Now that I had had some of my fur "loved off," I realized that my life was supposed to be about others. Now I was "real" too. When you carefully guard your image, you don't take risks to reach out to others; you dispense your time and love in tiny portions. Jesus was never like that. He lavished himself on the great strugglers of the world, those who wrestled and failed with their humanity. He talked to them, he listened and lovingly spoke the undiluted truth.

In his letter to the church in Thessalonica, Paul said, "We loved you so much that we were delighted to share with you not only the gospel of God but our lives as well" (1 Thessalonians 2:8).

Teach me to feel another's woe,
To hide the fault I see;
That mercy I to others show,
That mercy show to me.
ALEXANDER POPE

AN ANGEL'S MESSAGE

The older I get, the more I realize why God gave us each other, and why Paul spoke so powerfully about the body of Christ. I've learned that as I take the first step in reaching out to others, I receive back the grace I give. In the hospital I was lonely, so I befriended another lonely girl in our unit, and neither of us were alone. I was sad, and as I reached out to someone else who was crying, I was helped too. We need one another so much more than I ever realized. Sometimes help is standing right beside us, but because it does not look like what we prayed for, we can miss it. I almost did.

It was 1990. My life was very busy with ten live television shows a week. My secretary, Pat, was a gift from God. She could get through mountains of work and still remain calm and clearheaded. Every day, many people called asking to talk to me, and she was gifted in knowing which calls I should take and which could be handled by our team of counselors. One evening, when I was about to leave, she said there was a call she thought I should take.

Little did I know that an angel was on the line. I was familiar with some of the details of this woman's life because one of our field reporters had produced a feature segment on her. She had been raised in a very disturbed home, sexually abused by her mother and father. When a young teenager, she had hit the streets of Hollywood as a prostitute. Her street name was Angel, and she had a Mohawk haircut that was all the colors of the rainbow. Our introduction was a strange one. Angel and a friend had decided it would be fun to rip off a Christian bookstore. One of the tapes she stole that night was mine. She liked how I looked. My hair was short and spiky then, and because I was wearing a leather jacket, she decided to listen to my tape. (A bookstore in Dallas refused to stock that tape, because they thought I did not look like a Christian. Angel must have agreed!) She liked the music, and shortly after that she was invited to a church, where she gave her life to Christ. She wanted to get off the streets, but that's hard to do if it's the only life you've known. And for Angel, her street friends were her family.

Angel had written to me many times, so it was nice to finally put a voice to her letters. When she called that night, we talked for a long time. It was clear she wanted to live a new life, but she struggled daily to walk away from the drugs and alcohol that made her former life bearable. I made a commitment to her that day—that I would be there for her, to talk when she needed to. Over the next two years I saw her a number of times. She came to several concerts I gave in her area, and a couple of times she came to Virginia Beach. On one trip she was a guest on my show. It was so refreshing to have someone as honest and transparent as Angel; she gave us all a lot to think about. Whenever she phoned, I would pray with her and offer a few words of encouragement.

When I was released from the hospital, I met up with Angel again. It was incredible to see the growth and changes in her life (and in her hair color!). We talked about her life and how she was coping, and then she asked me how I was doing. I said I was fine.

She looked at me for a moment and said, "Why do you find it so hard to let people get close to you?"

I was surprised by her question. This was not how our relationship worked. I was the one who asked her questions and tried to help *her*. She smiled at my discomfort. "It's all right for you to need people too, Sheila," she said to me.

After I moved to L.A. in the spring of '93, Angel and I saw more of each other. I was amazed at her ability to deal with everything life threw at her. No matter what happened, she kept on walking with God. And drastic things did happen: Shortly after her decision to give her life to Christ, she was diagnosed with a brain tumor. The operation to remove the tumor was successful, but it resulted in a stroke, leaving the left side of her face paralyzed. Over time, she made a remarkable recovery; she fought hard to get well, which is why her phone call late in the summer of '94 devastated me.

"It's back," she said.

"What do you mean, it's back?" I asked.

"The tumor is back. I have another brain tumor."

I couldn't believe it. Why should one person have to endure so much? Angel had no family support, no loving mother to stand beside her all the way, as I had. She had just finished two years of hard work to recover from her last surgery. Having no money, she was sent to the welfare hospital in Los Angeles. I remember visiting her. When I think of a hospital, I think of pristine floors, clean white uniforms, and the utmost care given to the health and well-being of the patient. This place was another world. The bathroom I visited on my way to Angel's room was filthy—there were two huge cockroaches on the floor. Angel lay on a bed with one sheet over her. Through the open window, the dirt and smog of L.A. washed over her. She was too weak to speak, so I sat and held her hand. I talked to her doctor, who said he was pretty sure they had caught it all this time, but only time would tell.

The next day she seemed a little more lucid, and we were able to talk for a while. I left the hospital that day with tears burning my eyes and Angel's parting words searing my mind: "Can you imagine how awful it must be to be in here, Sheila, without Jesus? I am so blessed."

She fought hard again, through seemingly endless complications, and made it to the other side. As she became stronger and more independent, I called less often. Other issues were pressing at me, and my full schedule at school was demanding. I guess I thought she did not need me as much any more. Angel thought otherwise. She called me one day and asked if she could be candid.

"Please do," I said.

"I want to be your friend, Sheila, not your project. I think you need me just as much as I need you. If that's not what you want, then I will understand and walk away, but I want to be clear with you."

I didn't know what to say. Shocked by her words, I grew a little defensive, but one lesson I was learning was to really listen to people. She continued, "God has used you in my life in so many ways, and I will always be grateful for that, but I want to help you too."

I knew she was right. I viewed our relationship as a one-way street. God had used me to help her, and so I had adopted the role of expert. And now I was confronted with my arrogance. Here was a young woman who had faced so much sorrow in her life and yet, through the grace of God, she was walking close to him. She was taking a risk in confronting me, but she loved me enough to speak the truth. She was calling a spade a spade.

Angel's frankness reminded me of a story about a Christian school that placed a great emphasis on the Bible and learning the ways of God. An enthusiastic young teacher at this school was talking to her eight-year-old students. The teacher said, "Children, what is gray, has a bushy tail, eats nuts, and climbs trees?"

The class was silent.

"Come on, children," she encouraged. "This is not difficult. What is gray, has a big bushy tail, and gathers nuts?"

Again there was silence, until a little boy timidly raised his hand and said, "Well, I know that the answer is Jesus, but it sounds like a squirrel to me."

That's what I love about Angel—she calls a squirrel a squirrel!

More than that, Angel is a tangible answer to a specific prayer. I had asked God to weave me together with a few people with whom I could live the rest of my life. It is easy to pray heady prayers about the body of Christ, but it is wise to keep our eyes open, because sometimes the answers come in unexpected ways—they did with Angel.

POOR IN SPIRIT: THE FELLOWSHIP OF SUFFERING

The quote at the beginning of this chapter, from a member of Alcoholics Anonymous, is becoming more true for me every day.

> Religion is for those who are afraid of going to hell. Spirituality is for those who have been there.

Religion speaks of rules; spirituality speaks of life. I think of the parable of the rich man and Lazarus: The rich man had every luxury life would allow, and at his door lay a beggar who had nothing. For him a good day meant eating the crumbs that fell from the rich man's table; all he hoped for was a little mercy. The rich man knew the plight of the poor man, but he was deaf to his cries and blind to his desperate condition—until it was too late. When both men died, the poor man was carried to the final comfort and consolation of Abraham's bosom, and the rich man awoke to the burning torment of an eternal hell (Luke 16:19–31).

Jesus said, "Blessed are the poor in spirit, for theirs is the kingdom of heaven" (Matthew 5:3). Covered in the garments of religion, we are like the rich man in that we feel invincible, cushioned from the brokenness of the world. But true spirituality makes us poor in spirit; it brings us to our knees in wretched awareness of our sinful nature. We worship at the feet of the One who has made us clean—the One who took our suffering upon himself and in whose suffering we have fellowship. Philippians 3:10 says, "I want to know

Christ and the power of his resurrection and the fellowship of sharing in his sufferings."

The fellowship of suffering changes one's view forever—nothing looks the same anymore. The camera guys at CBN used to tease me about what they called my "mall ministry." Quite often, people who had seen me on television would stop me in the mall and talk for a while. Sometimes they would ask me to pray for a member of their families or for personal crises. It drove friends who were shopping with me nuts, but I saw it as part of my job.

Shortly after I was released from the hospital, I was wandering through the mall one evening looking for Christmas gifts for my family. I was standing at a counter, waiting to pay, when I realized someone was looking at me. I caught her eye and smiled, and she came over to me.

"I know you must be busy, and I don't want to keep you, but I would be very grateful if you could say a prayer for me if God brings me to your mind," she said. I looked into her eyes and saw such pain. I recognized that look of barely holding yourself together. "Do you have time for a cup of coffee?" I asked her. We sat down in a quiet corner, and she began to talk. She asked if I remembered reading about a terrible road accident the previous week.

Yes, I had been horrified at the loss of a man and two little children. "That was my family," she said. We sat there for a while holding hands, tears pouring down our cheeks. There was nothing to say, nothing that would make it any better. After a while, she dried her eyes and got up to leave. We embraced, and she looked deep into my eyes and thanked me. In one sense I didn't "do" anything. I didn't come up with any clever words or magic prayers. We had just sat for a while together, two people who love God, sharing the heartbreak of life and death.

The old Sheila would have prayed for that woman and hurried on, feeling self-satisfied that I had done a good thing.

But this time I really *saw* her, and we touched for a moment and left knowing our only hope is the Lord.

HEAR ME OUT

There is much in Scripture about listening to one another. And I've learned that when you are at peace with God and with yourself, you can extend grace to others who are in pain, even to those who snap at you.

After I had been at seminary for about a year, a friend asked if I would be a guest on a radio talk show. I wasn't sure I wanted to do anything in the public eye anymore—or if God wanted me to—but after consulting with close friends, we thought it would be good for me to accept this opportunity. There is still such a stigma attached to being in a psychiatric hospital that if even one person was helped by my story and the lessons I'd learned, then it would be time well spent.

So I went on the air. For the first hour everything went smoothly, and then I saw the interviewer frown and shake his head. When he threw to a commercial break, he told me they had a woman on hold who wanted to say something to me; she was angry. He said he was prepared to drop the call, but I asked him not to. I could not see any purpose in hiding from the genuine emotions of others. If she was angry with me, it would be better that she got it out than allow it to fester. When we were back on the air, they put the caller through.

"I am very angry with you," she said.

I could hear the emotion in her voice. In anger, she was very close to tears. "Can you tell me why?" I asked her.

"I certainly will," she said. "Is it true that you are divorced?"

"Yes, it is." I replied.

"I am so disappointed in you!" She began to weep.

"I understand that," I said quietly. "I am too."

I asked her if we could talk some more after I was off the air. She was obviously very distressed, and we needed some time. I finished the show. Later, from home, I called her, and we talked for a couple of hours. Her husband, a leader in a local church, had recently left her for another woman. After twenty years of marriage, he was gone, and she was left with a broken heart and unanswered questions. She was angry with me, she said, because "if people like you get divorced, perhaps it makes people like my husband think it is all right for them."

What could I say to her? She had every right to be angry. I simply listened and cried with her and told her how sorry I was. All that any of us can do is to live in line with the Word of God and keep our arms open to one another. At the end of our conversation, she was kind enough to say that she was not really angry with me; she was just very broken and very alone. She had needed a chance to speak, to be heard, to cry out, to beat her hands against the wall, to have someone hold onto her in the midst of her pain.

From that caller, I learned that we all need to hear beyond what is said to what remains unsaid just under the surface. This is a broken, fallen world, and we will fail one another miserably. But if we will learn to reach out to and hold on to each other through the maelstrom of words, we will find companionship on our journey that makes the dark days that much more bearable.

SOMEONE NEEDS TO TAKE THE FIRST STEP

It was always winter in the village, but no one seemed to mind. The memories of spring and summer were so distant, they sounded like a whisper from a pleasant dream.

The streets were lined with house after house, each with its own trim yard. Villagers smiled and greeted each other on the streets and talked to one another over their fences. No one was quite sure how it had happened, but those fences had become electrified—like the fences around a farmer's pasture. If you broke through the fence, the electric shock would jolt, maybe even kill you.

Village life was smooth and still. Very little happened to disturb the peace of the villagers' quiet lives. Oh, several years back there had been the incident with old Sam Hill's dog, but no one liked to talk about that anymore. Sam should have known better than to let the dog run free. At least the dog didn't suffer, they reasoned; the current had killed him quickly.

Sam's neighbor, Sara, was sad at the time, because she knew how much Sam had loved the animal. It had been his closest companion for years. But life moved on as it inevitably does.

Then one winter's day, a neighbor heard a strange noise coming from the bottom of Sara's garden. It was a low and constant moaning. People looked over her fence, and they were shocked by what they saw. Sara was lying in the snow, holding herself like a child, rocking back and forth, back and forth.

Some neighbors went back into their houses, convinced that Sara would not want them to see her "like that." A few stood and stared as if they had paid for tickets.

Then someone cried out, "Look at Sam! What's he doing? He's lost his mind."

Sam was walking toward Sara, heading for her yard.

"Stop, Sam!" they cried, but he was deaf to all but her cry. As he touched the fence, the current ran through him, but he kept walking until he reached Sara.

Then the strangest thing happened. As he sat beside her in the snow, cradling her in his arms, a shaft of sunlight broke through the cold, gray sky and rested on their heads.

"It could have killed you, Sam," Sara said.

"I know, my dear, but I knew that cry. I have heard it in my head for so long. I didn't know that you sang that song too. Let's go in now. I'll make tea." And that was just the beginning.

The world needs more Sams. How about you?

Dear Jesus,
You left behind the glory of heaven
to walk with us on earth.
As the current of our sin ripped through your heart,
forgiveness was on your lips.
Teach us to risk reaching out
to those who cry alone.
Teach us how to love.
Amen.

※

I tore down the dark and dismal drapes
that hung like dead men on the gallows.
I threw open the windows
and cried out as the sunlight spilled into this
silent room
as surprised as I.
And as my eyes became accustomed
to this fierce and searching light,
I realized it was time to laugh again.

※

10

Following the Shepherd

Men are disturbed not by things,
but by the view which they take of them.
EPICTETUS

I've read that Michelangelo was seen one day pushing a large rock down into his sculptor's "studio." His neighbors watched the ferocious effort he put into moving it, inch by inch. When one of the spectators asked him what he was doing, he replied, "There is an angel in here who wants to come out."

I believe that God will lovingly push us inch by inch to chip away the hard edges of our lives, to refine us into a work of art in which others will see his hand. Though such refining is never easy, it is what we were created for. Too often we settle for a mere existence when the hope of life in all its glory and pain is waiting inside the rock.

Just as Michelangelo's neighbors didn't see the hidden treasure before them, what we see—about ourselves, others, the past, the future—is often a matter of perspective. One night, while at a ballet, I sat behind a woman who I thought I recognized as a friend I had not seen for a while. I couldn't wait for the first intermission so I could surprise her. As the curtain fell, I tapped her on the shoulder and said

163

hello. When she turned around, I realized my mistake. She was a he! Seeing this person from a different angle, I realized he did not look anything like my friend. (She doesn't have a beard, for one thing!) A different angle further defined the truth. And so it is with life.

When I was eighteen, my favorite book was *Hinds Feet on High Places* by Hannah Hunnard. It tells the story of a young girl named Much Afraid, who chooses to leave the valley of fear where she has lived for years and follow the shepherd up into the mountain. Time after time she wants to stop and go back to the valley because the road ahead looks all wrong. Whether or not she continues her ascent up the mountain depends on whether or not she will trust the shepherd. Just before I left Virginia, a "700 Club" viewer sent me a new copy of that book, and I began to read it again. Suddenly, I saw myself in this young girl's position, full of fear, lacking in trust, subject to every wind blowing around her.

As I read, I took particular note of one thing: At every key point when Much Afraid chose to trust the shepherd and take one more step, the shepherd gave her a stone to keep. At the end of her long journey, when she finally "died to herself" and was given new legs to run with, she was taken—by two traveling companions, suffering and sorrow, chosen by the shepherd—to the top of the mountain. There she saw that each rough, colorless stone had become a beautiful jewel for her crown.

I believe that God, like the shepherd, would have us live trusting him at every turn. It was hard for me to let go, to truly trust Christ for my every breath, but as I continue on this journey now, I know as deep as the marrow in my bones there is no other way to live. What I used to know in my head, I now know in my heart. It is one thing to believe in the ability of a surgeon to perform life or death surgery on your body; it is quite another to allow yourself to be put to sleep and submit yourself to his knife.

As we trust, God is faithful to give us the spiritual rewards outlined in Psalm 23. I have loved this psalm since I was a child, when I learned to sing it to a wonderful old Scottish melody named "Crimmond."

In moving to California, I began to experience the Twenty-third Psalm in a new way. The territory was new. The road was scary. And at every turn God beckoned me to trust. He wouldn't let me down.

THE LORD IS MY SHEPHERD, I SHALL NOT BE IN WANT

As I prepared to leave Virginia Beach, it was sad to say good-bye to friends and colleagues, yet I felt anchored by a new hope I had not felt before. When you have faced the worst there is to know about yourself and experienced the gift of grace, life is new and wonderful.

In April '93, I had flown out to Los Angeles to sign up for school classes and to find a place to live. My search led me to a pretty apartment in Laguna Beach, close to the ocean.

On June 1, I left Virginia to drive to California. My friends were horrified that I was driving across the country by myself, but I was excited about the adventure. One friend baked enough cookies for the entire trip. Another taped herself reading stories to me, and one of my best friends (who had been Pat Robertson's security guard) gave me a baseball bat in case I ran into any trouble at a truck stop! I took five days to drive from coast to coast, stopping off to see friends in Indiana and Colorado. I enjoyed every moment of the trip.

I arrived in California with only enough furniture to fill a one-bedroom apartment and enough money to pay my rent and tuition for three months. In material terms, I was returning to the early days of my full-time ministry, when life had been a constant adventure of watching God faithfully provide not more than I needed and not less. Over the years I had accumulated a lot of "stuff" that demanded to be maintained. And while I knew the Lord was the giver of all that is good, I had lost that sense of depending upon him for my daily bread. Now I had left the "stuff" behind to live a simpler life.

Once in California, I still needed a few basics: a refrigerator, a washer, a dryer. I shopped around and the best price I could find was eighteen hundred dollars for the three. While that would have been nothing to me before, it now stood in front of me as a challenge. I asked the Lord to show me what to do. And he answered in a way I never expected. Before I had left for California, a friend in Virginia had asked if I would sing a song for a project he was working on for children in China. When he asked me if I had a fee, I said no, I wanted to do it simply because I believed in what he was doing.

Now, months later, I wandered down to my mail box in Laguna, enjoying the beautiful California sunshine, and found a letter from my friend. In it was a check for eighteen hundred dollars. The Lord had provided my need—to the dollar.

Just as David had recorded in the Twenty-third Psalm, I was able to say I was not in want because the Lord was my shepherd.

HE MAKES ME LIE DOWN IN GREEN PASTURES

Each morning in California I walked along the beach with the water lapping at my feet. I sat with a cup of coffee and my Bible on a favorite rock, bathing in the presence of the Lord.

To me, there has always been something very healing about the ocean. It speaks of the power and majesty of God, and yet as I watch it flowing gently over a rock, taking years to change its face, it reminds me of his tenderness and patience as well.

I found my new, simple life quite liberating. There's something very basic about "green pastures." Sometimes, however, we aren't content with green; we want "greener." Without realizing it, I had become consumed with things, using them to fill the emptiness inside me. Now I did not need to crave things, because the dark places in my life were being daily filled by the friendship of God.

I still spent time with a counselor, a godly, older woman. Each week we would look at what a Christian woman should be—how to be strong and yet gentle. I would wake up in the morning smiling, having slept all night with no bad dreams. Just as surely as God had led me to a dark valley, he was leading me to a place of peace and restoration.

HE GUIDES ME IN PATHS OF RIGHTEOUSNESS

I remember my first day of classes. Was I nervous! Since the class was at night, I had all day to "look forward" to the unknown. What if I couldn't make the grade? One of the aspects of clinical depression is the inability to concentrate; what if I couldn't do the work? There was only one way to find out.

I arrived on campus early, in case I couldn't find the right classroom. Carrying a clean, white legal pad and three new pens, I was the first to arrive. I had a choice of any seat, and took one near the back.

At exactly 6:30 P.M., Professor Nathan P. Feldmeth looked up and welcomed us to a new term of study. Then he led us in a prayer of thanksgiving for the privilege to be able to study and learn and grow. The class was in early church history. "This is our history," he said. "Let us start at the very beginning."

What a gift to someone who had lost her way! It might not sound appealing to some—to find yourself back in a classroom again—but I welcomed it. I was hungry to learn more about the ways of God, to rebuild my life on a solid foundation. I sat in that classroom overwhelmed by the goodness of God.

From that time on, each course I took put a piece in the puzzle for me: Christian ethics, the writings of C. S. Lewis, Paul and the church, the foundations of spiritual life. There could have been no greater gift than these classes were to me.

I worked hard and gave myself to the discipline of learning. And I had a lot to learn. When I did not know how to format a paper for a master's class, I found the professors more than willing to teach me, now that I was not afraid to be taught.

I surrounded myself with good books and good friends who shared a heart to become more like Christ. Although I was alone more than I have ever been, in the library, living alone, I was never, for a moment, lonely. Now that I had found my voice, I was able to ask for prayer or simply for company. As I immersed myself in the Bible, I formed a firm foundation for my life built on the character of God and not on anything I might have to offer. I felt whole. God was leading me on a new, right path.

I WILL FEAR NO EVIL, FOR YOU ARE WITH ME

When I had visited California in April to sign up for classes, a friend had called and asked me to stay a little longer and attend a "life-changing" seminar.

"I really think it would be good for you, Sheila," she said. "It has had a tremendous impact on our lives. Please say that you will think about it." She and her husband profusely recommended this seminar that had helped them discover who they were.

I assured her I would think about it, but after we said good-bye I was not sure I wanted to go to an intense four-day conference. I was tired of making changes. I had been out of the hospital only a little more than four months, and the thought of another life-changing event was a lot to swallow. But there had been something in my friend's voice that sounded different to me, and that difference was even more pronounced with her husband. He had always seemed a little cynical, but there had been no trace of that in his voice when we had spoken on the phone.

Even though I knew very little about the content of this seminar, I decided to go. I was to be at a hotel in Anaheim, close to Disneyland, by eight o'clock on Thursday morning. The conference would run through Sunday night. If it was too much for me, I figured I would just go and ride Space Mountain.

My friends had asked me to come with an open heart, prepared to get some feedback about my life. I was learning to be open to feedback, but it was still a relatively new concept to me. It had been my experience that if you appeared successful, people tended to come to you for advice. They don't usually take the risk of telling you where they think you need to shift your perspective. (Though perhaps I gave out signals that I was not open to that kind of input.)

On Thursday morning, I remember thinking to myself, *I hope this isn't a big cheerleading session where we all tell each other how wonderful we are.*

I should not have worried!

Forty of us sat in a circle. The instructor began: "This is not a seminar. This is your life. Who you really are will show up in this room at some point over the course of the next four days. You will receive from this experience exactly as much as you put in. Our purpose is to come to grips with what Christ meant when he said, 'Love the Lord your God with all your heart and with all your soul and with all your mind. . . . Love your neighbor as yourself'" (Matthew 22:37, 39).

Well, at least he uses the Bible, I thought.

The first day was spent responding to questions and choosing a team partner for the weekend. I chose a tall girl who had smiled from ear to ear since she'd walked in the door. Over the next four days, with our partners and with the larger group, we were given numerous opportunities to receive and give feedback about each other's perceived strengths and weaknesses.

A few of the lines of feedback I received included "You seem very angry" and "I see a mixture of strength and self-pity" and "You have compassion for others, but you are very wounded and you hold yourself back."

It was hard to listen to total strangers tell me my flaws. I would not recommend walking up to someone in the mall and asking what that person thinks of you, but in the context of this seminar—a controlled, supportive setting—I was willing and able to hear what was being said. I had prayed that morning that God would continue to teach me how to be more like Jesus, so I chose to stay open and not close down.

I was surprised at how accurate some of the observations were. I thought I had come *so far* in my growth, and yet I still had big strides to make. That weekend was not exactly "the valley of the shadow of death," but it was a valley of shadows—and in that valley God was with me.

In one of the days that followed we listened to a song called "Man of the Tombs" by Bob Bennet. The song told the story of a demon-possessed man chained outside a village. At times, in an intense rage, the man would burst the chains that held him. But even though he could break free of his external bonds, he could not free himself from the demon within. The point was clear: It is one thing to be *in trouble;* it is quite another when the trouble is *in you.*

Each word of this song spoke clearly to me, but one line pierced my heart: "He mistakes his freedom for being free." As I sat there listening, I saw myself clearly. A part of me was still bound by my tendency to hold other people responsible for what had happened to me. I realized that I alone was responsible for being apathetic about my life, discouraged, steeped in self-pity.

I got back to my room at eleven o'clock at night. Even though I was exhausted, I sat and thought for a while, reviewing my life through this new paradigm. I was where I was today by my own choices; no one else could be held responsible. It was as if my world was being turned on its head.

This new awareness of responsibility was bad news and good news rolled into one. It was bad news because I had to once again focus myself and take responsibility for my own life. It was good news because, if I was responsible for my present and future, then I could change.

It is very hard, sometimes painful, to change, but it is ultimately more painful to refuse to change. Can you imagine how sad it would be to lie on your deathbed full of regrets because you never had the courage to reach outside of your comfort zone?

In truth, I was angry. I had been feeling sorry for myself, and it had to stop. As I took in the truth that my sin held the Lamb of God pinned to a tree of torture, there was nothing left to say in my defense. All I could do was fall down on my face and worship as his blood washed over me.

I went to bed that night worn out, but strangely at peace. Facing what is true was both heartbreaking and liberating. There was no more need to hide or dress up my life or live alone. Rather, every day I knew I could bring my sinful nature to Christ in confession and ask him to continue to fill me with the Holy Spirit, transforming me into his image. In the valley, God was with me.

As the weekend progressed I threw myself into every part of it, aware that it was a gift to be able spend time with people who were also so committed to change.

YOUR ROD AND YOUR STAFF, THEY COMFORT ME

In Scripture, the rod is always used for correction. It is portrayed as the tool God uses to discipline his children. As a child I was spanked only twice that I can remember; both times I really deserved it. Yet, I knew without a doubt that my mother loved me—it was painful for her even to speak harshly to me—and I never made the same mistakes again. God does not turn a blind eye to the sin or foolishness of his children, but his discipline is just and merciful, and when it is over, if we have not stiffened our hearts in rebellion, we are changed; we look a little more like him.

I recently adopted an abandoned cat from the humane society. I call him Max. When Max was brought in by someone who had found him lying by the road, he was almost dead—unconscious and covered with blood. When I saw him he had just had his stitches removed and a drainage tube taken out of his back. What attracted me to him were his eyes. He has the kindest cat eyes I have ever seen. I asked if I could hold him, and he nestled in my arms, purring like an engine. I told the nurse I couldn't believe how sweet he was, and she replied, "The ones who have been through a lot are usually the most tender."

I took Max home with me. What a joy! Then one day, I noticed that he was walking with a limp—though he didn't seem to be in any pain. The vet explained that Max had torn a tendon. No, he wasn't in pain, and I had options. I could leave the leg as it was and Max would be fine, but he wouldn't be able to jump as high or run as fast as he had before. Or Max could undergo surgery and get the tendon repaired. I thought about the pain of putting him through another operation. Would it be worth it? I decided to go for it. After all, he had given me so much joy, he deserved the best that life could offer. The surgery would be incapacitating for a short time, but then Max would be back to his former self—able to do everything he set his sights on.

I saw parallels in my own life. While it is painful to allow God to perform surgery on our hearts, every time we submit to the knife, we become a little more like we were created to be.

God often allows other people to be part of the painful process of teaching us to be like him, but he does not take delight in the destruction of a brother or sister. It is clear that we are to hold one another accountable for our lives, but when discipline is necessary we are to do it with tears in our eyes. Because not one of us knows what tomorrow will bring, let us sow mercy in the lives of others, so that God will be merciful to us.

I painfully remember a dinner with my good friends Frank and Marlene at one of my favorite Laguna Beach restaurants. I love Indian food, and this particular place served some of the finest Indian cuisine I had ever tasted. During dinner, Frank said something I disagreed with and I told him so, strongly. After a few silent seconds, he said to me, "Do you know how it makes me feel when you talk to me like that?"

I said no.

He said, "I can't hear what you are saying because you are so angry; your anger is all I hear."

We were quiet for a while, and then I turned to Marlene and asked her what she thought. Marlene recounted a day trip the two of us had taken together, and asked me if I remembered what I said to her in the car park. I did remember—but my version was different from hers. My recollection was that she had said something I thought was out of line, and I told her so. She said, "I agree with you that what I said was probably wrong, but I do remember how stupid it made me feel to have you talk to me in the tone of voice that you used. You were so angry with me."

It was a sobering evening. When two people I love told me the same thing, it seemed wise to pay attention. I woke up the next morning to a beautiful day. I called a counselor and asked if it would be possible to "squeeze me in." Yes, she could. I told her what had happened the previous evening, and that I wanted to change, but felt stuck.

During the course of the next hour and a half, the counselor listened, asked questions, and provided some wonderful insight. One of the practical things she suggested was to write out the phrase "God loves a woman with a quiet and a gentle spirit." She told me to put it on my refrigerator door and pray for it every morning. I did that, and I believe God is helping me to change.

The turning point for me was listening to the input from people I love without being defensive. I realized I was what I call a "quiet terrorist," someone who didn't look like an angry person, but who liked to quietly control things from the sidelines. I now value genuine feedback from close friends very highly. People who love us want us to be the best people that we can be. Change is painful, but it gives birth to a new quality of life.

And it takes courage to confront one another in love. It is still hard for me at times to be as open as I need to be, but I work very hard at it. It is especially difficult for me to own up gently when I am upset with someone because my natural tendency is to say nothing. Of course, the anger eventually seeps out in subtle ways. I realize now that this is sin. When I harbor feelings in my heart that I don't lovingly tell the other person about, then I am controlling the situation rather than giving that person a chance to respond.

Still, I have to choose to do this. Some lessons I've learned are easy for me to act on, but this one is not. What I remind myself of in these situations is that it is God's expressed purpose for us to walk in the light with one another, so I do it—not because it feels good, but because it is right.

Friends who confront us with our weaknesses but never build us up are like "Job's comforters" who tear at us piece by piece. In his book *With Open Heart*, Michel Quoist tells of hearing the news that a good, generous friend of his had died, "defeated by depression." Quoist imagines what the funeral is going to be like and knows that praise will be heaped upon the dead man and his every virtue extolled. As he thinks about that scene, he says, "The tragic thing is that just a fraction of it [while he was alive] could have perhaps saved him."

We all need to hear encouragement. We need our strengths to be named and appreciated. On the other hand, friends who never speak what they perceive to be true about our sin or our failures are like tightly wrapped umbrellas that are full of holes: You think you can count on them until the rain begins to fall and you find yourself soaked to the skin. We need to love each other so actively that we speak both words of challenge and words of hope. In their book *Disciplines for the Inner Life*, Bob and Michael Benson say there is no truth toward Jesus without truth toward our fellowman. Untruthfulness destroys fellowship, but truth spoken in love cuts false fellowship to pieces and establishes genuine brotherhood.

In the psalmists' day, a shepherd's staff was used as a tool to guide and to lean on. It is one thing to believe that Christ carries a staff; it is another to lean on Christ and be held up. The hooked end of a staff also pulled a lamb back from the brink of disaster, nudging a straying lamb back on to the road, into the flock. The letter from the woman suffering with cancer that began my healing process in 1992 was, in a way, like the Shepherd's staff tugging at me. God in his grace nudged that woman to let me know that she *saw* me and knew I was in pain. I still have and treasure her letter, which is a comfort to me.

David states that he is comforted by both the rod and the staff of the shepherd. At one time I would not have understood that, because I viewed discipline as a pain to be avoided. Now I see that discipline is surely a gift to be treasured if I want to live a life pleasing to God.

YOU PREPARE A TABLE BEFORE ME IN THE PRESENCE OF MY ENEMIES

Let me take you back to the weekend conference where I first learned to accept feedback about my weaknesses. One of the final exercises of the conference was designed to have the group, who had been through a lot of intense exercises together, choose a leader. Everyone was required to cast a vote by giving a "yes" to the person he or she chose. As I stood there, one person after another came to me and said, "I choose you."

I did not want to be the leader. As far as I was concerned, those days were over. I just wanted to live quietly. One of the seminar leaders stood behind me as the numbers grew and asked me, "Are you listening?"

I was listening, but I did not know what to do with what I heard. I thought back to a movie I had recently watched called *The Mission*. In this film, Robert De Niro portrayed a man whose actions had led to the death of his brother. A consuming guilt ate at him like a cancer. Then he was given an opportunity to help some missionaries carry supplies to a new mission base at the top of a mountain. The climb was brutal and bloody, but he insisted on carrying all the supplies tied to his back. Each time he stumbled and slipped back down the unforgiving stone face, someone would offer to step in and help him carry his burden. But he always refused and continued to drag himself to the top of the mountain. As he reached the summit, a native Indian approached and cut his burden from him. As it rolled off his back, the old man looked into De Niro's face and began to laugh. De Niro too began to laugh, and laughed until he cried.

There comes a time when we have to let the past go. On the cross, Christ paid for our sin. He took our load upon himself. When we have received the grace to repent in brokenness, when we have done all that we can to right any wrong, we need to allow Christ to cut our burdens from us. We cannot be defined forever by our mistakes; rather, we need to be defined by the anointing hand of God, who calls us to worship him and serve him with humility.

As people placed their confidence in me that night, I knew I was loved and forgiven. But I hesitated to "hear" them, because I felt being forgiven did not mean I was ever to return to a leadership role. When I voiced that feeling to the man who stood at my shoulder, he said, "Are you insisting on being in control again, or are you willing to listen?"

I thought about what he said and realized one of my oldest fears was still at play—the fear of being rejected, of making enemies. If I simply removed myself from the game, then no one would have a chance to vote me out. I needed to stop protecting myself.

I decided, from this point on, to walk in honesty with others, knowing that some people would vote against me. If enemies rose, I would need to respond with humility, but not in fear. With a "table set before me in the presence of my enemies," I could hold my head high in the confidence of the Lord. First Peter 5:6 says, "Humble yourselves, therefore, under God's mighty hand, that he may lift you up in due time."

If others look to me to be a part of their journey—to be a leader—I do not have the right to walk away. I have to rely on the knowledge that Jesus is the one who places value on my life, no matter how good or bad others think I am.

As he lay in a Roman cell awaiting execution, Paul wrote to his friends in Philippi, "Rejoice in the Lord always. I will say it again: Rejoice! Let your gentleness be evident to all. The Lord is near. Do not be anxious about anything" (Philippians 4:4–6). Paul was in the clutches of Nero, an evil, brutish emperor who delighted in the suffering of others. History tells us Nero would hold feasts on the palace grounds and illumine the proceedings with the burning bodies of Christians. Yet Paul was not afraid of this petty potentate. He had been through the fires of suffering, and his sights were set on a land Nero could not touch.

First John 4:18 says that "perfect love drives out fear." God will do what it takes until that love is perfected in us. And as we listen, he will show us the next step in our ministry—the work he has anointed us to do—whether it is quietly singing songs to young lambs or publicly proclaiming his grace.

I've mentioned my friend Marlene. She is a constant encouragement to me to continue walking a transparent, simple life, humbly before God. One day Marlene called and

asked if I would be available to speak at a women's breakfast in Costa Mesa. I was hesitant, as it had been about two
years since I had been involved in any kind of public ministry. But Marlene, in her own unique way, reminded me we
are called to comfort one another in the same way we have
been comforted.

I said yes, and in faith I stood in front of this group of
beautifully groomed women, wondering if any of them
would be able to relate to my story at all. I told them about
my experience in the hospital and about the grace and
mercy of God as I faced my greatest fears. Tears flowed as
we drew closer to one another. It was different from anything I had experienced before. There was nothing standing
between those women and me. I was not "the expert." I was
a fellow pilgrim.

When the meeting was over, we stood and talked for a
while. One woman told me she had been struggling with
depression for years and had never told anyone. The woman
beside her gave her the name of a good Christian doctor.
Another told me her daughter was in a psychiatric hospital.
She had never shared this with others for prayer because
she felt it would stigmatize her child forever. We stopped
there and then and prayed for her. It was amazing to me to
be part of the body of Christ in action. I will never forget that
morning. It has multiplied over and over in other situations.

I would imagine that in your circle of friends or
acquaintances there are many who feel isolated, who long
to live an honest, transparent life before others and before
God. I know that wherever I speak or sing now, I am overwhelmed by the desire I see in people to live such a life. It
seems we are beginning to ask ourselves some of the more
important questions of life.

If you have "been through the valley," perhaps God has
anointed you to reach out and ask others around you to face
the important questions of life: Do you know who you are?
Do you long to say what you really think, rather than what

you think you should say? Do you ever ask yourself who your real friends are, because you keep your life so guarded? Are you enjoying the awesome freedom that comes from realizing that Christ knows everything about you and loves you passionately? Are you really living, or you just surviving?

AND I WILL DWELL IN THE HOUSE OF THE LORD FOREVER

The Twenty-third Psalm ends with these words: "Surely goodness and love will follow me all the days of my life, and I will dwell in the house of the LORD forever." What a promise! I begin each day with a prayer of thanks that I am living in the midst of God's abundant, full life. I have good friends who love me and whom I love. We speak the truth to one another and support one another. When the Lord brings to my mind something I need to "deal with," I make a commitment to do so at the first possible moment. When I find old resentments coming to the surface, I stop and immediately pray for that person, asking that God's mercy and grace will visit that person in ways he or she has never known before. My life feels light.

I have known the Twenty-third Psalm since I was a child, but now I know this psalm:

> *I whisper your name*
> *and before it sounds on my lips,*
> *you are here by my side.*
> *Too blind to see,*
> *too afraid to ask*
> *it took the loss of all I had*
> *to discover who I am.*
> *Some nights are darker than the sea bed*
>   *with no moon,*
> *but a stronger light*
> *that fits me like a baby in the womb*
> *moves me through the mist,*
> *and I would live a thousand nights without one star*

to know that when I whisper your name
here you are.

This earthly life is merely the overture to our eternal
life with Christ. Overtures give you a taste of what is to
come, but if you left the theater after these preliminary bars
of music, you would miss the masterpiece.

David was a man who trusted the Shepherd. That trust
and humility strengthened the very marrow in his bones. It
is a wonderful way to live. It brings dignity and peace to the
human heart. There is a poem that paints a passionate picture of the kind of man David was, the kind of woman I want
to be. I would love to share it with you.

IF

If you can keep your head when all about you
Are losing theirs and blaming it on you,
If you can trust yourself when all men doubt you
But make allowance for their doubting too,
If you can wait and not be tired by waiting,
Or being lied about, don't deal in lies,
Or being hated, don't give way to hating,
And yet don't look too good, nor talk too wise:

If you can dream—and not make dreams your master,
If you can think—and not make thoughts your aim;
If you can meet with Triumph and Disaster
And treat those two impostors just the same;
If you can bear to hear the truth you've spoken
Twisted by knaves to make a trap for fools,
Or watch the things you gave your life to, broken,
and stoop and build 'em up with worn out tools:

If you can make one heap of all your winnings
And risk it on one turn of pitch-and-toss,
And lose, and start again at your beginnings
And never breathe a word about the loss;
If you can force your heart and nerve and sinew

To serve your turn long after they are gone,
And so hold on when there is nothing in you
Except the Will which says to them: "Hold on!"

If you can talk with crowds and keep your virtue,
Or walk with King— nor lose the common touch,
If neither foes nor loving friends can hurt you;
If all men count with you, but not too much,
If you can fill the unforgiving minute
With sixty seconds' worth of distance run,

Yours is the Earth and everything that's in it,
And—what is more—you'll be a man, my son!
RUDYARD KIPLING

It came so soft one winter's night;
I never heard the door
or felt it dance into the room
and sail across the floor.
It crept upon my shoulder
and kissed me on the head,
and joy became a friend of mine
to call me from the dead.
For so long I have felt this need
but never knew its name
until its warmth began to melt
my snow-encrusted frame.
I see a look upon my face.
I know it came to stay.
I never will forget this winter's day.

11
The Incredible Lightness of Grace

*The word grace emphasizes at one and the same time
the helpless poverty of man,
and the limitless kindness of God.*

WILLIAM BARCLAY

Susan was very quiet at breakfast one morning. Her father asked if she was feeling all right, and she mumbled something under her breath and left the room.

"I don't know what has gotten into that girl lately," her father said anxiously to his older daughter.

"Oh, Dad," she said, "you are so blind when it comes to Susan. You always make excuses for her. She's a dreamer and she's lazy. She's always been lazy."

The father looked at his older daughter and smiled, "Perhaps you're right, Anne," he said, "but you have always been very hard on her."

"Well," Anne replied, "I don't have time to sit here and argue with you. I have a busy day. I'm meeting with the vineyard accountant this morning, and I am going to go over his books with a fine-tooth comb."

"But we have had the best year ever, and Peter is a family friend. I trust him completely."

Anne smiled as she looked down at her father, "That's why you need me, Father," she said as she left the room.

As he finished his coffee, he thought for the millionth time about the difference in his daughters—one weighed down by the world and the other carried on the wind.

He left the house, climbed into his Range Rover, and took off to look for Susan. He found her sitting under a tree, more asleep than awake.

"Susan, I know there is something on your mind. I wish you would talk to me," he said.

"I don't think you would understand, Dad," she replied.

"Why don't you give me a chance," her father said. "I love you."

Susan looked into her father's eyes, "I want to leave this place."

"What do you mean, you want to leave? Do you need a break?"

"It's not that, Dad," she said. "I know that when you are gone, Anne and I will be two of the wealthiest women in this area. You know Anne—she'll be quite happy sitting around in her slippers counting her money, but I want to do something now, while I'm still young enough to enjoy life."

Her father looked down at this daughter, so close to his heart, and asked her, "Is this—leaving—something you've been thinking about for a while?"

Susan was quiet for a moment and then she answered, "It's all I think about."

It was very quiet at dinner that evening. At the end of their meal, the father asked his daughters to bring their coffee into his study. He looked at the two faces, one so intense, one so restless.

"I have made a decision about my estate," he began. "We have done very well for several years in a row, and I have decided to sell some stocks and bonds and give Susan her share of the family money now."

"What?" Anne cried. "This has got to be a joke. She couldn't manage her allowance when she was ten years old!"

"I have made my decision, Anne," he said. "It will not affect you. Everything here will be yours. You will own the vineyard and all its assets."

Anne stormed toward door. As she left the room, she turned to Susan and said, "You are so selfish. All you think about is what makes you happy. Dad has poured his life into us and now you just walk out of here as if you own the world. I hope I never see you again as long as I live."

THE REALITY OF GRACE

The word *grace* is now as familiar to me as wind or rain, although, as a reality, it is something that was quite foreign to me until recently. Grace was never meant to be rationed, something we nibble on to get us through tough times. It is meant to soak us to (and through) the skin and fill us so full that we can hardly catch our breath. My problem was that I had such a tight grasp on my life, there was very little room into which grace could be poured.

The day I committed myself to the hospital, no one was more disappointed in me than I was. I had failed at my marriage, and I had let down people who were counting on me. I saw this same disappointment mirrored in the eyes of friends. I mulled over some of their words:

"Do you know the damage you are doing to this ministry?"

"I always knew you would lose it someday."

In the hospital, the doctor asked me what right I had to be angry with others who were disappointed in me. Wasn't I disappointed in myself?

Yes . . . and the thought was driving me deeper and deeper into despair.

Then came that glorious morning in a small church in Washington, D.C., when the pastor said, "There are some of you here today who feel like dead people staring up at the top of your own locked coffin. This morning, Jesus wants to set you free. You simply have to let go of the key and pass it through the little hole, where you see a tiny shaft of light."

I walked to the altar, dragging my shame and grief behind me. I knelt, with my head in my hands and lead weights on my feet, and, at the foot of the cross, confessed my utter hopelessness and helplessness to Christ and asked him to forgive me. At one point, I felt compelled to look up. As I did, it was as if Jesus himself were standing before me with outstretched arms, saying, "Welcome home, child, welcome home."

I stayed there for a while, basking in the radiant forgiveness being lavished upon me. It was one of the most humbling moments of my life. A gift had been given that would never be taken from me. I knew this to be true because I had done absolutely nothing to earn it, and it was given me in my most unlovable hour.

That afternoon, we were taken to a supermarket and given thirty minutes to shop. Supermarkets usually drive me nuts because there are so many things to choose from, but I didn't feel that way this time. I walked over to the fresh produce section and looked at the different kinds of apples. Everything seemed so wonderful! It was as if I had never been alive before. I wanted to hug myself, I felt so free.

Everything was different from that day on. I threw myself into the remaining weeks of therapy. Grace gave me the courage to face my biggest fears and the harshest truths about my life because it held on to me and never let go. I felt an overwhelming thankfulness deep in my bones. I knew I could never pay for this awesome gift, but it had my name on it, and it would never be taken away.

The joy that springs out of grace is so different from mere happiness. I was happy when my brother graduated with distinction from university. I am happy when I listen to my sister sing. It always makes me happy to talk to my mom. Happy occasions have always helped me forget about the things that make me sad. But the experience of joy is different, deeper, because it knows the whole story. Grace embraced all that was good and true and all that was bad and faithless about me. Grace is love with its eyes wide open.

True grace is so overwhelming you are compelled to extend it to those around you, whether they deserve it or not. George MacDonald said,

> Whether a man pays you what you count his debt or no you will be compelled to pay him all you owe him. If you owe him a pound and he owes you a million you must pay him the pound whether he pays you the million or not. If owing you love, he gives you hate you, owing him love, have yet to pay it.

That is a truly joyful and liberating way to live. Your mind is set; your path is clear; you need not depend on the reactions of others to determine how you will react to them because you have already made your choice. Grace takes the initiative to live with passion and compassion; it does not play it safe, but lavishes itself on others, just as grace is daily lavished on us.

Deep joy comes at unexpected moments. I felt it well up in me as I sat in my first class at seminary, but I also felt it when my friends lovingly challenged me about my attitude and my anger. I recognized the truth of their words and the correction of the Lord, and I am not afraid of either anymore; I hear both as a deep expression of love and commitment. I don't always welcome such correction immediately, but I hear it as a calling to be the person Jesus sees me to be.

This morning I watched a show on television that made me sad. The subject was teens who have no respect for their parents. A fourteen-year-old girl with a face of marble stated she hated her mother. The mother sat beside the girl and said she regretted the day she gave birth to her. As I looked into the eyes of the angry girl, I saw an angry but very scared child who had no anchor in this world. In the militant sixties we cried out for freedom, for no rules, for the right to live as we choose. And today the results of those terrible wishes are being played out in homes all across

America. St. Augustine said, "Thou hast made us for thyself, O Lord, and our hearts are restless till they rest in thee."

We were not made to live as unrelated beings, unaccountable and adrift. We were made for transparency and truth, for roots and friendship and community. This is possible only by the grace of God. There we find a place to make peace with ourselves—the good, the bad, and the ugly. I used to look at my reflection in the eyes of friendly people who did not really know me. What I saw was favorable, but it did not bring me joy because it was such an incomplete picture. Now I look at myself in the eyes of those who know me and love me, and I feel safe and grounded.

Grace is something that is deeply rooted in my mother, who gives freely out of a full heart. We had some tough times financially when I was growing up, but I can't remember ever worrying, because my mother carried her load lightly, dependent on and confident in the grace of God. She laughed with me and cried with me and cheered me on. When I made a bad decision, she reminded me of the mercy of God. She never shamed me but called me to keep pressing on.

Such fixed love and grace is a foretaste of heaven. I did not want anyone to write to me or call me when I was in the hospital, but the moment my mother said she wanted to fly over to be with me, I did not hesitate. I knew it would be painful for her to see me as I was, but I also knew she was unafraid of pain, and I welcomed her companionship. My heart truly breaks for those who have not experienced that kind of love in human flesh, but my prayer would be that you would find that love in God.

THE SECOND CHAPTER

Let's return for a moment to the story of Susan and Anne. Because of her father's generosity, Susan now had everything she'd ever dreamed of. She took a suite in the Beverly Hills Hotel and began to throw money around as if it were grains of sand. She waltzed down Rodeo Drive, enjoying the attention her lavish habits attracted. That night, she sat in the lobby bar sipping champagne, wondering what to do with her first night of real freedom. An exquisitely dressed man asked if he might sit with her, and she gladly said yes. They drank for a while, ate dinner, and then he suggested going back to her suite. Susan woke up the next morning with a pounding headache and a stranger beside her. She rolled out of bed and went into the bathroom to splash some water on her face. She looked at herself in the mirror and thought, "If Anne could see me now!"

Still laughing at the thought, she came back into the bedroom and ordered some black coffee and toast. When the stranger awoke, he showered and dressed. As he was leaving, he told Susan about a party that night in Malibu. He scribbled down the address and then was gone.

She went to the party. It was like nothing she had ever been to before. Music blared from the speakers around the pool, spilling out onto the beach. That night Susan was initiated into another world—a world of cocaine and hedonism. For six months she went to and gave the best parties. She woke up in a different place each morning.

But after two years, all her money was gone. Her inheritance had dripped away like snow in the sunshine, and with its demise her phone stopped ringing. She stood one morning looking at herself in the mirror of a cheap apartment. Her skin was sallow, and her hair hung limply on her thin shoulders. She thought of her father. She knew he would be heartbroken to see her like this. She wished she were home, but it was too late for that. She had ruined everything, and there was no going back. She remembered Anne's words and knew she would not be welcome.

TOO GOOD TO BE TRUE?

In his marvelous book *Shame and Grace*, Lewis Smedes tells the story of the day Robert E. Lee surrendered to Ulysses S. Grant. The defeated general expected to be humiliated and imprisoned along with his men. Instead, he was treated with dignity and respect. Grant told Lee to tell his men they could go home and that Lee, too, was free. As Lee mounted his horse to leave, Grant saluted him. Now that is grace!

When we come to the foot of the cross, we deserve to be shamed and rejected. Instead, we are forgiven, loved, and invited into the family. Does that sound too good to be true? It's too good *not* to be true! God has left us in no doubt.

> *My grace is sufficient for you, for my power is made perfect in weakness.*
>
> 2 CORINTHIANS 12:9

> *We are justified freely by his grace through the redemption that came by Christ Jesus.*
>
> ROMANS 3:24

> *It does not, therefore, depend on man's desire or effort, but on God's mercy.*
>
> ROMANS 9:16

I love to look at old family photographs. I have one favorite of my sister and me. She is about four, and I am about two. There is such a look of life in our eyes, as if it had never crossed our minds that we were anything but two of the niftiest kids on the planet. Grace gifts us with that child-like security that everything is going to be all right.

I recently hosted a television special featuring a man who has a remarkable ministry in India. I wanted to familiarize myself with a glimpse of the religious climate in that exotic and overpopulated country, so they sent me a film to review. I was shocked by footage that included seated men with knives through their cheeks or metal hooks in their chests in an attempt to please and appease their multitude of gods. The men worshiped at temples, with rats crawling all over them. They degraded themselves in any way imaginable in order to earn favor with stone statues that brought them no comfort in this world or the next. Contrast that scene to true grace: There is nothing that you or I can do to make ourselves worthy of the gift of grace. We cannot earn what was born in the heart of God.

Grace is not meant for only special occasions. I still tease my mom about her "good" clothes. When she buys a new suit or dress, it will hang in her wardrobe for eons, waiting for just the right occasion. I, on the other hand, most often try to squeeze into a new outfit in the car on my way home from the store. God's grace is not a suit meant for Sundays; we should wrap it around our shoulders every day of our lives.

I read a story the other day about a severely disfigured man who falls in love with a beautiful young woman. He is so ashamed of his appearance, he wears a mask to cover his entire face. Over time he wins the heart of the woman because he is kind and gentle and loves her so completely. They live happily together for many years, until she asks him to take off the mask. He is afraid of revealing his ugliness to his beautiful wife, but she is determined to know him fully. He stands before a mirror and slowly peels this facade away. Astonishingly, when it is removed, there are no scars. He had been made whole by his wife's unconditional love. In the same way, through the sacrifice of Jesus, God does not see the ugliness of our fallen humanity when he looks at us; instead, he sees the beauty of his Son.

There is a bakery in Laguna Beach that makes the best peanut butter pie on the planet. When I go in, I always look to see who is behind the counter. My heart sinks if it is the younger woman who works there, because she cuts such small pieces. But if it is the older woman, my heart sings. She lives life generously, and this attitude is reflected in her pie cutting. There is nothing stingy about this woman. She smiles not only with her eyes and her face, but with her whole body. Even though I don't know much about her, she has the look of someone who has weathered some storms in her time and emerged a stronger, more tender woman with a big heart.

Can you imagine how the world would be transformed if we all chose to live with gracious, generous hearts? Can you imagine the peace we would encounter if we set aside our petty differences and narrow-minded prejudices and embraced one another as we have been embraced by Christ? This kind of living would transform everything it came in contact with. Consider the woman who broke her jar of expensive perfume over the feet of Jesus. Even though she was criticized by others for the recklessness of her act, Christ reprimanded her critics, telling them they did not understand what she had done. There is no better moment to pour your love out on another. *Carpe diem:* Seize the day!

I treasure my volumes of the collected sermons of Charles Spurgeon, who spoke about grace with such depth and simplicity. He described returning home one evening after a very busy day when he was suddenly confronted by the text, "My grace is sufficient for thee." He thought about the words for a while, and then their meaning came to him in a new way: "MY grace is sufficient for thee." He said he burst out laughing, it was so clear. "It seemed to make unbelief so absurd," he wrote,

> It was as though some little fish, being very thirsty, was troubled about drinking the river dry. The river said, "Drink away little fish, my stream is sufficient for thee." Little faith will bring your souls to heaven but great faith will bring heaven to your souls.

All we have to do is humble ourselves before God. As we move toward him, we will see him running to meet us. That's what happened to Susan.

COMING HOME

She was so tired. She had walked for miles, catching an occasional ride from a stranger. She rehearsed her words over again in her head: "Dad, I know I have blown it, and I don't expect you to forgive me. I would just be very grateful if you would let me work in your office."

Back at her father's house, Anne was standing at the property line, talking to her father about increasing the price of this year's chardonnay. She could tell her dad was not listening.

"What's wrong, Dad?" she asked.

"Look," he cried, "in the distance, doesn't that look like Susan?"

Anne could only see the dust. Suddenly her father took off running, as if his very life depended on it.

Still down the road from the gate, Susan's eyes were downcast, but she looked up as she heard a noise growing louder, nearer.

She stopped dead in her tracks when she saw it was her father running toward her. When he was just a few feet away, she began her prepared speech. "Dad, I know that I ..."

She was cut off in midsentence as her father threw his arms around her and spun her in the air, his tears washing over her dusty neck.

"Welcome home, Susan. I've been waiting for you every day." There was no "Where have you been?" or "Why didn't you call?" There was only the outpouring of love from a father to his daughter.

Anne, however, had a much different reaction to her sister's return. "I can't believe you, Father," she said angrily. "This idiot leaves here and wastes all the money you and I have worked so hard for, and then she just shows up, looking like a wreck, and you expect me to be happy?" Her whole body shook.

"Listen, Anne," the father replied, "I thought your sister was dead, but she has come back to us. Everything here is yours. Can't you just be happy that our family is whole again?"

"I have stayed by your side and worked twelve hours a day to make this business run smoothly," she cried. "You expect me to be happy that the one person who let us all down is home? That is not fair, Father."

"This is not about *fair*, Anne," he said. "This is about family."

WELCOME HOME, CHILDREN

You probably recognize this story as a retelling of Jesus' wonderful parable about the prodigal son, who left and then returned home. The world is full of "grace robbers" like the prodigal son's brother and Susan's sister Anne, but we mustn't let them rob us of the joy that comes from being welcomed home by our Father. When God gives us new coats to wear, we shouldn't let anyone pull our old rags out of the trash. Just as we are, right now, God could not love us more. He is inviting us to join the swelling numbers of people around the world who have renewed their commitment to loving one another as they have been loved, and who have determined to extend to one another the grace that has been lavished on them. God reminds us to look back to that tiny stable two thousand years ago where, as Chuck Swindoll has written in *Grace Awakening*, "On that first Christmas morning, when Mary first unwrapped God's indescribable Gift, grace awakened."

If you have lived for years under the exhausting burden of guilt for having left home and squandered your inheritance, it is time to return to the Father whose arms beckon you home. Grace may have awakened on Christmas morning, but our redemption was completed in Christ's death and resurrection. We may feel incredibly unworthy (and we are), but we must remember that God loved us so much "he gave his one and only Son, that whoever believes in him shall not perish but have eternal life" (John 3:16).

I think again of the movie *The Mission,* and the look on Robert De Niro's face as his merciless burden rolled down the hill. Suddenly his life was light again, and this same joy is waiting for us too if we will just bathe ourselves in the incredible lightness of grace.

> *At the cross, at the cross where I first saw the light,*
> *And the burden of my heart rolled away,*
> *It was there by faith I received my sight,*
> *And now I am happy [joyful!] all the day!*
> ISAAC WATTS

> *Gracious Father,*
> *where do I even begin to thank you for the love*
>   *and mercy and grace you have*
> *showered upon me?*
> *You exchanged my heaviness for a lighter life,*
> *my sorrow for joy,*
> *my shame for love and acceptance.*
> *Help me to be a channel of that grace that came*
>   *to stay.*
> *Amen.*

～

Master strokes across a faceless canvas—
bold moves, color splashes over stones,
unfettered, young, full of dreams.
Beneath his brush the impossible comes to life,
awesome and intimate.
I stand amazed, silenced by the gift;
then he dips my finger in the paint
and I become part of the picture.
I feel so small.
It's like finger painting with Picasso,
but as God takes my hand
the paint on his melds with mine.
A new color is born.

～

12

Stand Up and Walk

There must be always remaining in every man's life
place for the singing of angels.

HOWARD THURMAN

A young boy stood and stared at the door for a while, wondering what it looked like on the other side. He pressed his ear to the wooden entrance and listened, but he couldn't hear a thing.

I want to knock and go in, he thought, *but I can't do that until I know my name.* He knew the ancient story that the one who lived behind the castle door was the one who gave life meaning. But how could he approach the wise one if he did not know his own name?

The boy fell asleep by the doorway. The next morning, he set off to find out what his name was. He ran into two of his school friends and asked them, "Do you know my name?"

They looked at him, then at each other, and walked away laughing.

He went into the little church on the edge of the village green and asked if he could speak to the minister.

"I'm sorry, Son, he is very busy," said a woman who was arranging flowers.

"But you don't understand," the boy said. "It's important. I want to ask him if he knows my name."

"That's quite enough of that nonsense," said the flower lady. "Now run along."

The boy sat by the bank of the river and looked at his reflection in the water. Tears rolled down his cheeks, and he felt somewhat hopeless. People either did not know his name or were not going to tell him. He lay for a while, sobbing into the soft grass. Then he jumped at the touch of a hand on his shoulder. He looked up. To his surprise, he was back at the door, and it was open. He looked at himself, covered in grass stains, with mud on his knees. He had planned to wear a new suit to meet the wise one, once he had learned his name.

He knocked very quietly on the unlatched door, and a voice like music told him to come in. He saw the owner of the castle standing by a window, looking out over the village. "I, um, I didn't want to come until I knew my name, but . . ." Unable to finish speaking, the boy stood with his head bowed, tears dripping on his shoes.

The man walked over to the boy and put his arms around him. "My son," the man said, "if you wanted to know your name, you should have come here first. I am the only one who can tell you. After all, I am the one who gave you your name."

LOOKING FOR "ME" IN ALL THE WRONG PLACES

This boy's story is like my own. I have chased the world looking for the answer to the basic question of who I am. It seems crazy to me now that I did not think of going to God alone to find out who I am. But like the boy in the story, I had such a desire to please him that I wanted to have everything in place before I really presented myself. For a long time, I thought my salvation rested in making myself useful to the Lord and that somehow, by spiritual osmosis, I would find myself in the process. Part of that is true; we are blessed by helping others. But like most lies, which start with something true but then get distorted, my good intentions led me astray. The more I tried to "give out" even as my own well was running dry, the more the "real me" disappeared. In time, all that was left was a smiling plaster shell.

I remember how I felt when I read the first review of my debut album. It was a very favorable critique, and I read each line as if the reviewer were talking about someone else, not me. When it sunk in that they were talking about me, I pasted the bits that made me feel good onto some of the emptiness in my heart. Later, when it became clear that the BBC show was going to be a success, the British TV Guide did a two-page story on "Scottish girl makes it big in London." People began to stop me on the streets and ask for my autograph. I was now the girl on television. This persona was much bigger than me, and I felt a little lost in her shoes.

When I moved to America, my life became much more complicated. I love this country, but I am very disturbed by the way Americans view success, particularly in the church. As I became well known, especially after I moved to Christian television, I was looked on as a "special" kind of Christian, a cut above the rest. My persona was the perfect place to hide. I didn't have to wonder who I was—everyone knew. Yet, like many successful people, I was miserable on the inside, because I had no real sense of self. It was as if I had lots of beautiful threads, but no fabric to hold them together.

I often look at my mother as someone who is as firm as a rock and who knows who she is. She struggled through the loss of her husband in his thirties and devoted herself to raising three children under the nurture and care of God. I used to wonder if she were miserable and simply putting on a brave face for us, but I know now that is not true. I have come to the conclusion that there is nothing more important in this world than to be at peace with the Lord and yourself—and she is.

HONESTLY

I started out on this journey with the best intentions in the world—to love and serve God—but somehow, somewhere, I took a wrong turn and got lost. When I was a teenager, I knew I was in a lot of pain inside, but I did not have a clue what to do about it. I decided my mother had enough to worry about without dealing with my unnamed feelings. I know she tried to reach me, but I decided silence was my best defense. Emotionally, I had fallen down a well, and I couldn't climb out. I relate that time in my life to a line by Norman Cousins, who wrote, "The tragedy of life is not in the fact of death, but in what dies in us while we live."

I can look at several points in my life where the Lord gave me an opportunity to get help, but I did not. I was too afraid. I believed that if I let others into the deepest parts of my life, I would lose myself. I know now that that is not true. The only way for me to find my way back home was the destruction of the fragile mountain I had built around myself.

FALLEN CASTLES

A long time ago, in a country far away, a dark, bleak castle sat high on a mountain. The wind sounded like tears as it wrapped around the castle walls. Though they never heard her, the villagers below the castle knew a young girl lived deep inside the granite walls. She'd built the fortress herself. Every spring the girl would walk down to the waterfall in the village square and sit for a while. Out here in the open the people would approach her and talk to her about their lives, but they were never invited to the castle. Then, as suddenly as she had appeared, she would be gone, encased again in her tomb of stone.

One day the village people awoke to a terrible noise coming from the castle. It sounded as if all the wind and rain and thunder in the world had gathered there, and above it all they heard a cry more terrible than anything that had ever tumbled down the steep mountainside.

The people gathered in the village square and listened. Suddenly the castle walls shook and great cracks ran through its granite walls. "What shall we do?" they asked. "We know the girl is in there."

"There is nothing to be done," said the village elder. "We must wait."

All day long the cries continued as, stone by stone, the castle fell into pieces. For three days, the castle crumbled. Some people left, feeling the girl had brought it on herself; others watched, fascinated by the spectacle. A few stood side by side with tears running down their cheeks.

At the end of the third day, the castle was little more than a pile of dust. The tear-stained villagers climbed the mountain. At what was once the castle door, they saw a body lying deathly still. The elder stooped down and picked up the girl. She was still alive, though for days she lay in a deep sleep somewhere between death and life. Finally, one day she opened her eyes.

The villagers knew the castle had taken the girl years to build, each stone resting on the next. It had meant so much to her. Should they tell her it was gone?

The elder spoke tenderly. "We do not know what happened, my dear, but it is all gone."

She looked at the group gathered around, taking in every face, and then she smiled. "I know it is gone," she said. "I pulled out the first stone."

That is how my life seemed to me. What had looked like a castle had been a self-made prison separating me from the rest of the world. The first stone pulled out of my castle wall was a desperate cry to God for help. He was not sentimental about the walls I had erected around me; he allowed the castle to crumble in order to save the life of my lonely, walled-in soul.

WHO I AM

I know that, as a human being, I am made in the image of God. That truth is like a river that steers me through my life. Because of the sacrifice of Christ, I am forgiven for my sins and restored to fellowship with God. This covenant engraved into the hand of God is secure; it is eternal. As a child of God and a member of the body of Christ, I belong with the fellowship of believers. We are family forever.

People were made for community. While it is wonderful to have a home to love, a place of peace, we often use that place of rest as a place to hide, to isolate ourselves from one another. But homes are not eternal. Relationships are the only things that have eternity written all over them. We need to "find ourselves" in Christ and in relationship with one another. It is in relationship that we see our strengths and our weaknesses and find the courage to change.

Have you ever thought that you would not know who you were if what you did for a living was taken away from you? Often, it is not until we lose our jobs and our homes and all of our "stuff," that we see clearly who we really are. For me, it was as if Jesus had walked into the temple courtyard of my life and turned over the tables. As the dust settled and I surveyed the broken pieces all around me, I knew this might be my last chance to walk away from what was not real and find what was.

NEW OPENNESS

When I think back to my 1993 move to California, I remember those first few days so well. I had arrived two months before classes began so I could settle into my apartment. It was such a happy feeling to open the door and walk into the freshly painted shell of my new home.

I sat on the floor by the window and poured out my heart to God. I thanked him for giving me safety on my cross-country journey and for his constant companionship. Everything was new. It was as if I had been born all over again, with only a few scars to remind me of where I had been.

Just hours later, the movers arrived with my furniture. As they brought in the boxes, I unpacked them. They teased me about all the books I had as they carried box after heavy box into the apartment. I offered to make them lunch, and we sat down on the floor to eat. I was filled again with a sense of the dignity of human life. As we broke bread together, I wondered about their stories. It is so easy not to see people, to rush past with no eye contact, guarded and insulated from life. I thought about the men in the homeless shelter I drove past every day in Virginia Beach as I rushed to get to my "safe" studio—where no one could touch me—to talk about the love of God.

I thanked the moving men for their kindness as they left, and they shook my hand and wished me happiness. I slept like a baby that first night and woke to the sun streaming through my window.

My first prayer request after I arrived in California was for God to give me a friend. I knew how important it was for me to be connected to the body of Christ. One day I received a call from a woman who said she had heard I had moved to town; did I want to have dinner sometime? I had never met her, though we had several mutual friends.

The first night I met Marlene, I knew I had found a friend. She was real, and said what she thought without measuring it out slowly to gauge my reaction. It was obvious that she had a passion for Christ, and she made me laugh. What more could I have asked God for?

NEW DISCIPLINES

It had taken me a long time to come to that place of quiet inside. In that place I found the invigorating value of the disciplines of solitude, fasting, meditation, and prayer. As I said earlier, I had fasted before, but only as a desperate attempt to find God in the midst of clinging to "religion." Fasting, for me, was like the waving arms of a drowning woman, never an offering to God or a heart-response of obedience to a call to fast.

I had spent a lot of time alone before, but I was never quiet. My meditations were interrupted by the sense that I had no self inside. I had to look in the mirror to see if I was there. Like the boy in the story who waited outside the castle door, when I prayed, I stood outside, refusing the invitation to come in because my dress was dirty.

What had been on the outside of my life was so noisy and "present" that it had become the whole song. Now all of that was gone, and the new song Jesus put in my heart came from inside. As part of my life, I began to take time out to be quiet, to listen, to let my heart and mind slow down for a while.

I've thought about what my friend at CBN said to me before I left for Washington, "Be careful or you might never be that special Sheila Walsh again." She was right! I am no longer "special" in the way that I had been, and I am glad!

RUNNING FREE—FOR A PURPOSE

When we left the Velveteen Rabbit, he was learning what it cost to become real and the pain of the process. He was also about to discover what a rabbit was made for. He did become the boy's favorite toy, occupying the place of most importance in the nursery. But one day, the boy became sick with scarlet fever.

Some adult came through and cleaned out the nursery, tossing the rabbit out in a sack of rubbish to be burned the next morning. As he lay in the sack, the rabbit wondered what use it was to be loved if it ended like this. A real tear ran down his velvet face, and a flower sprouted where it fell. Out of the blossom stepped the nursery fairy who carried the rabbit off to a place where all the "loved, real" toys lived. She put him down on the grass and told him to run.

> He found that he actually had hind legs!
> He gave one leap and the joy of using those hind legs was so great that he went springing about the turf on them.

He was a Real Rabbit, at last, at home with the
other rabbits.

This beautiful children's story contains many profound
truths. It is painful to go through the process of becoming a
transparent, authentic human being. It takes time, and we do
not control its schedule; that is in the hands of God. At times,
it seems as if the process is shut down and we are abandoned
in the darkest night of our lives. Each step takes courage and
faith to keep walking, especially when it looks as if the road is
leading us back to roads we have walked before. In the end,
however, we begin to understand what we were created for.
As we continue to walk, we find others who have been made
real as well, and the journey continues with them.

Jesus did not set me free so I could wallow for the rest
of my life in my new freedom and joy, but rather so the grace
and space that had been gifted to me would be shared with
those around me.

TO COMFORT AS WE HAVE BEEN COMFORTED

Dietrich Bonhoeffer was one of the few voices to speak
out against Adolf Hitler's maniacal plan for Europe. When
Hitler came to power, Bonhoeffer left Germany and pastored
a church in England. But when he received a call to return to
his homeland to head up a seminary for young pastors, he
accepted the call. There he refined his teaching on community
(which has been published and is left to us), but at a price to
himself: On April 8, 1945, he was hanged in Flossenburg for
refusing to bow the knee to anyone but Christ.

Bonhoeffer recorded that all Christian community
springs out of the truth that we belong to each other only
through and in Jesus Christ. Richard Foster, in his book
Devotional Classics, quotes Bonhoeffer:

> The Christian lives wholly by the truth of God's
> word in Christ Jesus. If someone asks him, "Where is
> your salvation, your righteousness?" he can never

point to himself, he points to the word of God in Christ
Jesus which assures him salvation and righteousness.

As we gather together, we meet one another as carriers of the message of salvation, speaking what is true again and again as we are faced with a world of lies and confusion. What we have received from God, we extend to one another. That is why there is no hope for peace or grace outside of Christ: We can only give what we have been given. As Bonhoeffer writes, "Our community with one another consists solely in what Christ has done to both of us."

If we begin to view our brothers and sisters as those in whom Christ actually dwells, I believe we will behave differently toward one another. As I reflect on the many bitter squabbles that take place within the church, I realize we all need to have our hearts broken by God. Arrogance and divisive behavior have no place in his kingdom, but they will stay with us until we humble ourselves before God and get a clear picture of ourselves.

Jesus told his friends not to be concerned about the speck in a brother's eye, but rather to take care of the logs in their own eyes. I used to find that difficult to understand. It was clear to me how it would apply in certain circumstances, but not always. Having been dealt with by God, that verse reads very differently to me now. When I find myself becoming angered by the behavior of others, it is usually a good sign that I had better pay attention to something in my own life. So often we attack others because of what we see of our own flawed humanity in them.

I read somewhere of a young man who, when he told his rabbi he really loved him, the rabbi replied by asking, "Do you know what hurts me?" Confused, the young man asked why the rabbi posed such an irrelevant question. The old man looked at his enthusiastic student and replied, "How can you love me, if you do not know what hurts me?"

NO NEED TO SCRAMBLE FOR FIRST PLACE

There is an event held every summer in Estes Park, Colorado, for the Christian music community. The day schedule features seminars and competitions for up-and-coming artists, and at night concerts are given by established artists. If you're on at night, you get twenty minutes to showcase your music. The tension backstage is ridiculous. We artists get up onstage as if we all needed brain transplants and there is only one brain available—which will be awarded to the artist who gets the longest standing ovation.

What used to happen to me up in that thin mountain air was that I wanted to be *the one* whom God spoke through. Now, it is good and right to pray that God will move among and speak to his people, but to long to be *the* one through whom he speaks—as if that would make that person seem more spiritual to others—is an erroneous concept. We can dance through hoops for one another, raise the dead, and speak with the eloquence and authority of a prophet, but if we do not love each other, we are simply a noise in God's ears. Elizabeth O'Connor said it so beautifully in *Journey Inward, Journey Outward:*

> Whether a man arrives or does not arrive at his own destiny . . . depends on whether or not he finds the Kingdom within and hears the call to wholeness—or holiness. . . . He does not have to scramble for a place in the scheme of things. He knows that there is a place which is his. . . . Life becomes his vocation.

CHALLENGE

God gives each one of us unlimited resources in Christ to rise above small earthbound dreams and to live lives that reflect eternity in our hearts. But it is hard, even heartbreaking sometimes, to step out from behind our masks and be known. But even though it is hard now, it will be much harder if we leave it until later. In *Mere Christianity*, C. S.

Lewis wrote that "the cowardly thing is also the most dangerous thing." He used the example of a mountain climber facing a climbing task that is very hard to do, but is also the safest thing to do. If he bypasses it, hours later he will be in far worse danger. He goes on to say,

> It may be hard for an egg to turn into a bird: it would be a jolly sight harder for it to learn to fly while remaining an egg. We are like eggs at present. And you cannot go on indefinitely being just an ordinary, decent egg. We must be hatched or go bad.

When there is something physically wrong with our bodies, we accept that, to be healthy, we have to deal with the problem. People who ignore the body's warning signs don't always get a chance to live to regret it.

It is the same with our hearts and our souls. God in his compassion gives us signs that all is not well, but it is much easier to ignore them and just keep walking. A sickness in our souls is much more dangerous than a weak heart or a few cancer cells. I do not want for a moment to minimize the pain and trauma of disease, but when our hearts are at peace in Christ, we can say with Paul, "For me to live is Christ, to die is gain" (Philippians 1:21). What is most tragic is to never really live at all. Perhaps your own path is strewn with the garbage of the past. Many adults today are held hostage by childhood traumas with which they cannot make peace.

I ask you with all my heart to open yourself to embarking on the only journey that leads to life. As long as you have breath in your body it is never too late. If, like me, you have buried your anger and shame for so long that you are severely depressed, there are many wonderful Christian treatment centers and godly counselors available. Or ask a trusted friend to recommend someone. There is nothing to be ashamed about in reaching out for help. It takes a lot more courage to step out into the darkness than to stay in the prison in which you may currently be living.

By the same token, if your husband or wife or someone you love is in trouble, you should reach out to him or her as well. Sometimes we are afraid to reach out in case we cannot put the pieces back together again, but it is much worse to deny a problem until the whole thing explodes and the pieces are scattered to the far corners of the earth.

One of the letters I received after appearing on "The 700 Club" to say good-bye was from a well-known Christian speaker who wrote to me from a drug and alcohol rehab center. He said he had lived in misery for years, torn between the success of his work and the devastation in his private life. He wanted to get help many times, but knew it might cost him everything. He had finally found the strength to walk away from the addictive spotlight to a place where he could be made whole. His letter reminded me of the words of the martyr Jim Elliot: "He is no fool who gives what he cannot keep, to gain what he cannot lose."

All human platforms and the trappings of success will one day be left behind and only things built in honesty and integrity with Christ will endure.

THE ESSENCE OF LIFE

I know that someday I will stand before almighty God and give an account of my life. I have made many mistakes that Christ has graciously covered with his blood, but the greatest mistake of all would have been to ignore the call to come out of the darkness and show myself. We can continue to take care of the outside of our lives, or we can turn away from what will not last and ask the Lord to show us who we really are.

I spent a lot of time grieving over the picture of who I am without Christ. I will not forget it, and I have asked God in his mercy to never let me banish that picture from my mind. It may seem like a nightmare to face all that is true about ourselves, but when we combine it with the glory of who we are in Christ, it is a gift that will take us through the night until the morning breaks.

During the course of writing this book, I was invited to speak and sing at a retreat for staff and key supporters of the ministry of my good friend Joni Eareckson Tada. In the worship service on the final morning, a man slowly made his way to the podium to read the Scripture. Born with cerebral palsy, he had been through years of speech therapy and was now willing to read in public. He read from 2 Corinthians 12:7–9: "There was given me a thorn in my flesh, a messenger of Satan, to torment me. Three times I pleaded with the Lord to take it away from me. But he said to me, 'My grace is sufficient for you, for my power is made perfect in weakness.'"

As I listened to this man read, I saw with my own eyes the truth of those verses lived out in front of me. Flying home that day I realized that we are all disabled; it is just more noticeable with some of us than others. Some of us are blind or in wheelchairs, while others of us are angry and bitter. What matters now is what we are going to do with our disabilities. If the man who had battled cerebral palsy had kept himself locked away, embarrassed by his disability, he would never have brought so much to us during the service that day. Only in surrendering ourselves to living transparent, accountable lives, can we be God's picture show to each other and to the world—a visible, tangible demonstration that God is real.

I know it is hard to change after having lived one way for so long, but it is not too late; you just have to seize the moment and begin. You are not alone. Christ will be with you every step of the way. There is a place for each person that no one else can fill, and there is something you bring with you, when you step out of the shadows, that no one else can bring. Perhaps like me before I began my own journey, you feel you are locked inside a prison. But just beyond those prison doors there are people who are cheering you on. If you'll just try the door, I think you'll find that it is open.

Prayers are heard when children pray,
though sometimes it takes years
to find the strength to listen
to the truth behind the tears.
Her body grew, as children do;
inside she lived alone,
a little girl,
her spirit bruised and trapped beneath a stone.
But one day in her prison cell,
a tiny shaft of light
began to burst through bars of steel
and lift the dead of night.
And as the little girl looked up
she saw herself all grown,
and the hand she took
that led her out
looked strangely like her own.

The man at the pool of Siloam waited for thirty-seven years for someone *else* to help him. Then Jesus came along and said to him, "Rise up and walk." Often, we have wasted much of our lives waiting for someone else to take that first step of healing for us. I say to you, in Jesus' name, "Rise up and walk! Come out of the shadows, step into the light. You were not created to merely survive, you were made to LIVE!"

EPILOGUE

I woke up to a beautiful December morning with the sun shining softly through the windows of my room. It was December 3, 1994. I lay awake for a while listening to the sounds of the street below. Christmas shoppers were out in force , and I could hear Bing Crosby singing "O Little Town of Bethlehem" as the music drifted up from the hotel lobby beneath my room. I looked at the beautiful dress that was hanging on the outside of the wardrobe and the silver slippers on the floor. Today I would be married in Charleston, South Carolina, to a wonderful man, a true gift from God. We had chosen this elegant city as it was where Barry, my husband to be, was born.

I thought back to the rehearsal dinner of the previous evening and smiled. The room had been filled with people who knew us well. Barry's mother's speech was so forthright and funny that she stole the show. My family and close friends had flown in from the United Kingdom for the wedding and as my brother, Stephen, spoke in my father's place, I was reminded of how rich I truly am. I have a family who loves me unreservedly, a man whose kindness and strength have won my heart, and a future secure in the grace and mercy of a Father who sees all, who knows all, and who loves us all.

I am grateful for a new season, a new beginning in my life. As I take this step into the future, I pray that God will use the lessons of the last years to shape our marriage, to sustain us as we serve him, and to help us live a life worthy of his calling.

If you are interested in having Sheila Walsh speak at your church, conference or special event, please contact her office at:

P.O. Box 150783
Nashville, TN 37215

Gifts for Your Soul
Sheila Walsh

This book of devotional meditations will nourish your hunger for deeper intimacy with God. Sheila Walsh turns her attention to the basic truths of the Christian life. Honest and refreshing, Sheila's writing encourages readers to exchange life in a spiritual rut for a renewed passion for Christ. She says, "I spent so many years on the external surface of my life that my inner life became weed-choked and overgrown. That is why I wrote this book. Not because I have great answers but because I have a great hunger to know God, to learn how to love, to care for the part of my life that is eternal."

Here's what readers of this great devotional are saying...

If you've read *Honestly,* you know Sheila speaks truth that grips your soul. In *Gifts for Your Soul* she goes deep, and the words are even richer. Her work is a gift in the midst of the struggles and realities of life.

Stephen Arterburn
Cofounder and Chairman, New Life Clinics

One of Sheila's most fetching qualities is her ability to present material with a freshness and newness that draws the reader closer to the Lord. Her thoughts, vibrant and simple, show great compassion and empathy.

Barbara Johnson
Spatula Ministries

Sheila's insights on forgiveness and grace were especially meaningful for me. Follow her toward Jesus—and unwrap gifts for your own soul.

Patsy Clairmont
Best-selling author and speaker

Gifts for Your Soul is packaged in a size that makes it perfect for gift giving and devotional use. Pick up your copy at a local Christian bookstore.

Gifts for Your Soul - Hardcover
ISBN: 0-310-20975-7

We want to hear from you. Please send your comments about this
book to us in care of the address below. Thank you.

ZondervanPublishingHouse
Grand Rapids, Michigan 49530
http://www.zondervan.com